Spiritual Care
in Our Multifaith World

Spiritual Care
in Our Multifaith World

A Primer on Practice and Theory

DANIEL S. SCHIPANI

WIPF & STOCK · Eugene, Oregon

SPIRITUAL CARE IN OUR MULTIFAITH WORLD
A Primer on Practice and Theory

Copyright © 2024 Daniel S. Schipani. All rights reserved. Except for brief quotations in critical publications or reviews, no part of this book may be reproduced in any manner without prior written permission from the publisher. Write: Permissions, Wipf and Stock Publishers, 199 W. 8th Ave., Suite 3, Eugene, OR 97401.

Wipf & Stock
An Imprint of Wipf and Stock Publishers
199 W. 8th Ave., Suite 3
Eugene, OR 97401

www.wipfandstock.com

PAPERBACK ISBN: 978-1-6667-3156-9
HARDCOVER ISBN: 978-1-6667-2422-6
EBOOK ISBN: 978-1-6667-2423-3

VERSION NUMBER 07/16/24

Scripture quotations are taken from the New Revised Standard Version Bible, copyright (c) 1989 National Council of Churches of Christ in the United States of America. Used by permission. All rights reserved worldwide.

Contents

Gratitudes | vii

Introduction | ix

1   Understanding Interfaith Spiritual Care | 1

2   Engaging the *Spirit* in Spiritual Care | 20

3   Common Ground: Community, Wisdom, and Discernment | 40

4   Spiritual Distress: Toxicity, Struggle, and Injury | 60

5   Strategies and Approaches in Interfaith Spiritual Care | 88

6   Fostering Interfaith Competence: A Journey toward Proficiency | 107

Bibliography | 129

Gratitudes

MANY PEOPLE HAVE CONTRIBUTED to the making of this book, beginning with a large number of counselees and other care receivers, students, and supervisees in diverse cultural contexts and settings. I continue to learn the art of spiritual care with and from them.

My gratitude also goes to colleagues and friends, too many to name, on five continents. Their collaborative spirit, encouragement, and gentle challenge is truly invaluable. Within that group I especially recognize the members of the International Association for Spiritual Care and the Society for Intercultural and Interreligious Pastoral Care and Counseling.

I also thank the administrators, faculty, and especially the doctoral students at three theological schools with which I have been associated as an affiliate professor of pastoral and spiritual care for several years: McCormick Theological Seminary, San Francisco Theological Seminary, and Seminario Teológico Centroamericano in Guatemala. They have helped me to articulate much of the content of this book.

During the last decades, Anabaptist Mennonite Biblical Seminary has been my academic home. I'm grateful for the unfailing support I receive from President David Boshart and Academic Dean Beverly Lapp. I appreciate ongoing conversations and collaboration with faculty members, especially professor Leah Thomas, and Jewel Gingerich Longenecker and Dan Schrock, Director and Curriculum Specialist of the Doctor of Ministry program, respectively. I also treasure immeasurable assistance from several people and places in the institution: Karl Stutzman, Director of Library Services, and his staff in our wonderful library; Brent Graber, Director of Information Technology, and his team; research assistant Chialis Thuan; copy editor Laura Campbell Rhoades; and Volunteer Coordinator Ed Kauffman.

The final words of gratitude go to both my "spiritual" and "biological" families. I'm deeply thankful for the nurture, guidance, and accountability structure provided by my local faith community, and by my spiritual director in particular. And I'm most grateful for the sustaining love of my wife and our children and grandchildren. My spouse, Margaret, is the quintessential wise caregiver who knows how to provide space for those around her to flourish. I dedicate this book to her.

Introduction

THE CONTENTS OF THIS BOOK stem from years of clinical work, teaching and supervision, research, and collegial consultation and collaboration in diverse contexts and settings in Latin and North America, the Caribbean, and Europe. In my vocational journey, the overarching epistemological and methodological framework has been supplied by practical theology; in other words, action research that is empirically grounded, interdisciplinary, hermeneutically structured, normatively infused, and pragmatically and strategically oriented.[1] Furthermore, those practical and theoretical endeavors have been carried out with a Christian perspective on care and justice that informs both a vision of reality and normative criteria regarding human life in community.[2] From that religious and theological *location* I address the question, "What is spiritual care?" However, before I offer a response, the following paragraphs discuss an ongoing worldwide transition in nomenclature—from "pastoral" to "spiritual" care—in healthcare centers, educational programs, and pertinent literature.

"Spiritual care" is increasingly used in connection with chaplaincy, and with Western clinical and academic settings, in particular.[3] In these settings, the qualifier "spiritually integrated" is associated with psychotherapy or counseling.[4] "Pastoral care" and "pastoral care and counseling"

---

1. Osmer, *Practical Theology*; see also Miller-McLemore, *Christian Theology in Practice*; and Swinton, *Practical Theology and Qualitative Research*.

2. From a philosophy of science viewpoint, practical disciplines concerned with the orientation and reorientation of human behavior, such as education and psychotherapy, cannot be ethically neutral. They always involve visions of reality and normative criteria concerning "good" society, "healthy" human life, and way(s) "forward" in human development, whether explicitly or implicitly. For example, Don S. Browning systematically unveiled the implicit metaphysical and ethical assumptions of major modern psychologies in *Religious Thought and the Modern Psychologies*. My Christian perspective is represented in the writings of pastoral theologians such as Ryan Lamothe in *Care of Souls, Care of Polis*; and *Radical Political Theology*.

3. See Cadge and Rambo, *Chaplaincy and Spiritual Care*.

4. Kenneth I. Pargament envisioned spiritually integrated psychotherapy as psycho-spiritual care that is explicitly attentive to life's existential dimension and necessarily pluralistic, integrative, and value-laden. Pargament, *Spiritually Integrated Psychotherapy*, 17–23. See also Richards et al., *Handbook of Spiritually Integrated Psychotherapies*;

continue to be used primarily in reference to caregiving offered within, or on behalf of, religious communities and institutions. At the same time, especially in the United States, "pastoral counseling" has evolved as a distinct professional practice in relation to increased religious diversity, changes in managed care, and technological capabilities that connect people across sociocultural divides.[5] In any case, it is undoubtedly necessary to foster commitment to linguistic hospitality and semantic clarity within diversity, while seeking to build common ground in communication and collaboration across cultural contexts, traditions, and disciplines.

Generally speaking, the shift to "spiritual" care correlates with ongoing sociocultural developments in religion and spirituality in late modern societies. Attention to the related processes of deinstitutionalization and pluralization helps us to appreciate the significance of social changes taking place in our time, while also illuminating the challenges and opportunities of caregiving in multifaith and multicultural contexts.[6] "Deinstitutionalization" refers to the process through which the traditional religious institutions, especially Christian ones, lose control over the religious and spiritual dimensions of society and culture. "Pluralization" refers to the increasing diversity of religious and spiritual traditions and perspectives. "Multifaith" is here used descriptively to denote the presence of a plurality of traditions (that is, religious and non-religious beliefs and value systems such as in Buddhism and Humanism) in a given social context. "Interfaith" connotes dynamic interaction between persons of different faith or spiritual traditions.[7]

Sandage and Strawn, *Spiritual Diversity in Psychotherapy*.

5. For a comprehensive survey of multiple voices and views that reflect the current status and possible way forward for pastoral counseling as a discipline, see Maynard and Snodgrass, *Understanding Pastoral Counseling*.

6. See Schipani and Bueckert, *Interfaith Spiritual Care*; Weiß et al., *Handbuch Interreligiöse Seelsorge*; Schipani, *Multifaith Views in Spiritual Care*; Schipani et al., *Where Are We?*; Noth and Reichenbach, *Pastoral and Spiritual Care*; Snodgrass, *The Art of Spiritual Care Across Religious Difference*; Liefbroer, *Interfaith Spiritual Care*; and Weiss et al., *Care, Healing, and Human Wellbeing*.

7. Readers should keep in mind a rule of thumb concerning the connection between *intercultural* and *interfaith* caregiving: All clinical and other learnings stemming from reflective practice and research in the field of intercultural care and counseling also pertain to interfaith care and counseling. Systematic writings on the former came first, however. See Augsburger, *Pastoral Counseling Across Cultures*; Lartey, *In Living Color*; Federschmidt et al, *Handbuch Interkulturelle Seelsorge*; Pedersen, *Counseling Across Cultures*; and Sue et. al., *Counseling the Culturally Diverse*.

INTRODUCTION

Connected to deinstitutionalization and pluralization, we often meet people self-defined as "spiritual but not religious,"[8] as well as increased religious and spiritual fluidity and hybridity—that is, multiple religious belonging.[9] To some extent in response to those trends within the overarching socio-economic and cultural globalization process underway, we also recognize and confront religious and political fundamentalism.[10]

It is with awareness of such complex and challenging realities that I invite readers to reflect on spiritual care in multifaith contexts, and to encourage dialogue and collaboration among representatives of diverse traditions, cultures, and disciplines. The section that follows is a proposed five-point response to the question, "What is spiritual care?"

SPIRITUAL CARE ACROSS TRADITIONS, CULTURES, AND DISCIPLINES: GUIDELINES FOR UNDERSTANDING AND PRACTICE

- Human life has a *spiritual dimension* (or "human spirit") that is biopsychologically grounded and socioculturally fashioned. It manifests itself as a longing for wisdom patterned with a search for meaning and truth, connectedness and communion, purpose and vocation. On the one hand, the spiritual dimension confronts spiritual (or "existential") threats such as meaninglessness and emptiness, condemnation and alienation, and despair and sense of "lostness."[11] On the other hand, spiritual growth and revitalization (or "inner healing") defines a flourishing life with enhanced creativity and character hallmarks such as love, peace, joy, generosity, courage, and more.

- Diverse spiritual and religious traditions have explicitly addressed the spiritual dimension and its existential quests throughout millennia, as documented in sacred texts and other artifacts. They can be called *wisdom traditions* because they offer paths toward growth in wisdom (or "spiritual-moral intelligence") and human wholeness. Philosophical

---

8. See Mercadante, *Belief Without Borders*; and Quack et al., *Diversity of Nonreligion*.
9. See Bidwell, *When One Religion Isn't Enough*; and Barnett, *Christian and Sikh*.
10. The theme of fundamentalism as toxic spirituality is included in chapter 4.
11. "Spiritual dimension" (and "spirituality," for that matter) is not a synonym for "religious dimension" (or "religiosity"). The category of spiritual dimension may include religion however viewed, experienced, and practiced, but not necessarily so.

INTRODUCTION

and theological traditions started much later to also explicitly address the spiritual dimension. Further, the systematic study of, and explicit engagement with, the spiritual dimension in the social and behavioral sciences, and clinical psychology in particular, is relatively recent.

- Throughout the ages and across cultures, diverse forms of caregiving practice have been available in order to focus on, engage, guide, support, reorient, and/or heal the human spirit thus understood. Fundamentally, *as a compassionate response to human suffering,*[12] *spiritual care is a special way (process) of companioning; and all forms of spiritual care have always involved connecting wisdom traditions with care receivers' spiritual resources, longings, and struggles in socio-culturally and contextually pertinent ways.* Such can be, therefore, an acceptable response to the question, "*What is spiritual care?*" Multiple forms of dialogical-narrative and hermeneutical process (i.e., discernment as practical wisdom) are normally involved in those ways of companioning.

- Given that "psychological" and "spiritual" are inseparable in real life, such understanding and practice of spiritual care can be articulated as *psycho-spiritual care*[13] and applied to the whole group of "helping professions" (counseling, psychotherapy, life coaching, medicine, ministry broadly speaking [e.g., pastoral care and counseling, chaplaincy in diverse settings], nursing, etc.). The caregiving process focuses on and engages the spiritual dimension in light of the resources of diverse wisdom traditions, including nowadays those of psychology and other behavioral and social sciences.

- A holistic approach in caregiving practice and theory is a special contribution of spiritual caregivers involved in all of the healthcare disciplines. They can consistently demonstrate holistic spiritual caregiving competence. Competence can be described and assessed with a profile of interrelated sets of distinct competencies in the domains of knowledge and ways of knowing, personal character, and multiple

---

12. In this context and broadly speaking, *suffering* can be understood as "dis-ease"—that is, "disturbance of ease" in situations ranging from mild disorientation to severe trauma.

13. "Psycho-spiritually" here refers to the realms of emotions, feelings, thoughts, and behaviors together with people's "faith" or "spirituality," however understood and practiced and/or their worldview and life commitments, also however understood and enacted.

INTRODUCTION

caregiving skills. Competencies in turn correlate with standards, that is, expectations of caregiving excellence on the part of institutions and programs and, especially, the care receivers themselves. Further, spiritual caregivers must be able to navigate cultural and spiritual-religious difference amidst growing global pluralization and an increasing number of multifaith contexts and settings.

The systematic explication of these guidelines by this book stems primarily, although not exclusively, from a Christian theological perspective.[14] Chapter 1 presents an overview of necessary practical and theoretical considerations for interfaith caregiving situations. Chapter 2 offers a comprehensive proposal for understanding and engaging "spirit" and "spiritual" in caregiving work. It is followed in chapter 3 by a discussion of community, wisdom, and discernment as key areas of common ground shared by diverse traditions that inform and guide spiritual care. Chapter 4 deals with spiritual distress and harm manifested in fundamentalist and authoritarian toxicity, and in spiritual and moral struggle and injury. Strategies and approaches in the face of religious difference is the focus of chapter 5, followed by a detailed examination of competence in interfaith spiritual care in chapter 6.

In the last several years, the growth in research, theory building, and enhanced clinical practice in spiritual care have been remarkable. Readers will find in this book numerous references to the writings of colleagues representing different religious and theological traditions. Correlated to those developments is the design of new programs to educate professional spiritual caregivers to work competently in increasingly "secular" and multifaith settings and social contexts. Another priority being addressed is care for people who represent particular religious traditions and/or belong to faith communities, and also for those self-described as spiritually "hybrid," "fluid," and/or "non-religious." There is a twofold movement in that direction, particularly in the North Atlantic. On the one hand, in addition to programs associated with the Christian faith, others are connected with certain traditions, such as Jewish, Islamic, Buddhist, and Hindu. They prepare caregivers primarily, although not exclusively, for *intra-faith* spiritual care. Those programs also seek to equip students for *interfaith* work carried

14. The fruits of earlier research on interfaith spiritual care were published in Bueckert and Schipani, *Spiritual Caregivers in the Hospital*; Schipani and Bueckert, *Interfaith Spiritual Care*; and Schipani, *Multifaith Views in Spiritual Care*. Chapters 1, 2, and 6 of this book include updated and expanded versions of material previously published.

INTRODUCTION

out from the perspective of their particular tradition. On the other hand, new initiatives are also emerging that focus primarily on interfaith care broadly speaking, especially in university settings and medical centers; they can also offer the option for students to further their training within their own tradition.

In addition to curriculum development and the strengthening of clinical practice as such, progress is noticeable regarding the specific dynamics of intercultural and interfaith clinical supervision. This agenda includes the variables involved in the supervisory relationship itself, as well as the consideration of group dynamics that foster intercultural and interfaith competency. Further movement is also happening concerning systematic research and evidence-based articulation of theory as a necessary complement to qualitative methodology.[15]

In light of these ongoing developments, this short volume is intended as a companion text or complementary resource. It was written with the purpose of encouraging further reflection and dialogue among chaplains,[16] pastors and other religious caregivers, Clinical Pastoral Education and psychospiritual therapy[17] students, counselors, psychotherapists, and others interested in the field of spiritual care in our multifaith world. It is released with the hope-filled expectation that spiritual care theory and practice across traditions and disciplines will continue to be enhanced in the days ahead.

---

15. For almost three decades, George Fitchett has been a leading advocate for evidence-based spiritual care in healthcare chaplaincy. See Fitchett et al., *Evidence-Based Healthcare Chaplaincy*; and Nolan and Damen, *Transforming Chaplaincy*.

16. The name "chaplain" is still widely used in English-speaking parts of the world. In some settings in the United States, Canada, and elsewhere, the word is being replaced by "spiritual care (or spiritual health) specialist (or provider or professional)" and "spiritual caregiver."

17. The Canadian Association for Spiritual Care (CASC/ACSS) certifies psychospiritual therapists who "use interventions informed by spirituality, religion, and psychology as well as counseling theories, ethical standards, human diversity and the range of human traditions."

1

Understanding Interfaith Spiritual Care

THIS CHAPTER OFFERS AN overview of the challenges and opportunities that we face today in different kinds of interfaith care situations. Practitioners, researchers, teachers, and supervisors would agree that any list of essential tasks for interfaith ministers, counselors, psychotherapists, chaplains, and others must include those listed below:

- Understanding how personal and communal belief systems relate to physical, emotional, and spiritual health and healing, holistically viewed.
- Connecting with the spiritual reality of care receivers as revealed by them, in order to address collaboratively their needs, longings, and potential.
- Engaging as a witnessing, listening presence while accompanying care receivers in caregiving processes aimed at sustaining, guiding, empowering, liberating, restoring, and healing.
- Encouraging and enabling care receivers to mobilize their spiritual resources in their own way, on their own terms.
- Helping healthcare team colleagues, both narrowly (e.g., in the hospital setting, counseling programs, etc.) and broadly speaking, to understand and contribute to holistic caregiving practice and theory.

In light of these and related tasks, this chapter pursues three interconnected objectives: to identify key issues relevant to interfaith spiritual care; to propose a model for interdisciplinary reflection and caregiving practice; and to foster collegial conversation and collaborative research aimed at improving overall interfaith spiritual care competence.

The first section consists of a case study from healthcare chaplaincy practice. It is the story of a caregiver who is an atheist and discovers the value of prayer in an interfaith encounter. The chaplain's testimony is examined as an exercise in practical theology, with its fourfold epistemological structure and methodological dimensions: empirical-descriptive (observation), interpretive (analysis), normative (evaluation), and pragmatic-strategic (application).[1] The second section of the chapter presents key features of interfaith spiritual care as a relatively new and rapidly growing sub-discipline. It does so by highlighting the unique contributions of spiritual caregivers and the necessary place and role of interdisciplinary perspectives. It also proposes a four-dimensional framework for spiritual care theory and practice.

CASE STUDY: AN ATHEIST PRAYS WITH HOSPITAL PATIENTS AND RELATIVES

Chaplain Sally Fritsche's reflection on her personal story and vocation as a spiritual caregiver[2] supplies an interesting window into the promise and possibilities of a transcultural and transreligious approach to spiritual care. Following the excerpts below that document her transforming encounter with the family of a dying man and her own spiritual journey leading up to it, there will be a brief analysis of her experience.

> Meeting Ernesto was the beginning of a shift in my feelings on how an atheist might pray. . . . It was one of my first shifts as a chaplain at Brigham and Women's Hospital in Boston, and a nurse called to say that a Catholic man was nearing the end of his life, and his family wanted someone to come say some prayers. I was the only chaplain on call, so I went.
>
> The small hospital room was crowded with easily 15 people, Ernesto's bed in the center. His wife was there, his children and

---

1. See Osmer, *Practical Theology*. For a presentation demonstrating the structural analogy between the case study method and practical theology as a discipline, see Schipani, "Case Study Method," 89–101. The article includes an interfaith spiritual care illustration involving a Christian (Baptist) chaplain caring for a Jewish family. See also Swinton and Mowat, *Practical Theology and Qualitative Research*.

The value of case studies for research, training, supervision, and collegial collaboration in healthcare chaplaincy is illustrated in Fitchett and Nolan, *Spiritual Care in Practice*; and Fitchett and Nolan, *Case Studies in Spiritual Care*. See also Kruizinga et al., *Learning from Case Studies*.

2. Fritsche, "An Atheist's Prayer." Fritsche is currently the associate minister for congregational life at the Unitarian Universalist Church of Urbana-Champaign, Illinois. I am grateful for her permission to include her essay as a case study and for fruitful conversation with her on related issues of shared interest.

cousins and brothers, his grandchildren. I was prepared to hold their sadness and anger, to offer support and affirmation of their grief. But I couldn't imagine how I was going to pray. I didn't want to lie to these people. . . . (They want me to talk to God for them, but won't a prayer from me be empty? Won't the words come out meaningless? Won't it feel like a lie on my tongue? But a dozen pairs of teary eyes turned to me.)

I invited everyone to gather close and reach out for each other and, together, we prayed the Hail Mary, the Our Father, and prayed for whatever comes next to come with peace and overwhelming love. And those prayers, those prayers were far from empty.

I came into the room wanting to help, and expecting to feel helpless. I came with skepticism, ready to say the words of Catholic prayers if they wanted them, but not expecting those words to come from my heart, or to become a truly spiritual experience. But joining my voice with the sobs of those at their father's deathbed, and saying the words, "Our Father, who art in heaven . . ." I didn't have to believe we were talking to God to see something real in that.

Those prayers were deeply healing, not just for the believers in the room, but for me, too.

Observation

Chaplain Fritsche grew up Unitarian Universalist. At home, she had been encouraged to experiment with prayer, meditation, and different kinds of spirituality:

> I went to church, to mass, to Hindu temple, to synagogue, and to my mid-Missouri town's lone mosque. And . . . I loved it. I loved religion wherever I found it. I coughed through the incense, fumbled the right-to-left prayer books, and soaked in the powerful peace that can happen when faith communities come together. . . . The problem was, when I looked honestly into my own heart, there just wasn't any "religion" there in the way I had been taught to think about it. When it comes down to it, I lack, quite simply and sincerely, any belief in God, an afterlife, or anything not earthly, observable. . . . I never intended to be an atheist, but here I am. My love of religion, my commitment to religious community, and my personal atheism exist side by side, deep and unforced, beliefs that I find written into my very bones.

The chaplain has always loved religion but had never prayed as a religious practice. She always viewed prayer critically and had been convinced that she could never pray sincerely. It would be expected, therefore, that prayer and praying would present a special challenge both personally and professionally. In her own words again:

> Given my non-belief, prayer has never meant a lot to me. Can an atheist pray? Or perhaps more importantly, why would an atheist want to? . . . When I came to terms with my lack of belief in God, I never felt like I was missing out on much by missing out on prayer. Even the more thoughtful approaches to prayer haven't gotten through to me. . . . With no God, what's the difference between *prayer* and just reflecting on a concept in the privacy of your own head? And when I need help, or want to express gratitude, it would feel silly to turn to a listening ear I don't believe actually exists. Why pray when no one's there to hear me?
>
> So prayer, I've gradually come to realize, just isn't for atheists like me. And that's fine. There are other ways I connect to the sublime and the sacred, but without a belief in God, prayer can't really be one of them.

Analysis

Chaplain Fritsche recognized that her encounter with Ernesto and his Catholic family was a turning point for her, both vocationally and professionally. She discovered that she can actually pray meaningfully and, in her words, "from the heart" in ways that are timely and effective. Let us consider what was going on, and why, by listening to her own version of the experience:

> So what, exactly, was happening when I prayed for Ernesto and his family? This isn't a conversion story about an atheist who sees the error of her ways and the power of the Lord. I wasn't praying to any God, but I was praying. And there was *something* powerful happening in that room. Something about the end of a life, the family's intense need, the connection formed when they reached for me, the chaplain, asking me to carry their sadness and their hopes, asking me to help them put it all into words and to tell their God what they need.
>
> Ernesto and his family were the first people I prayed for in the hospital, but they were far from the last. In my work as a chaplain, I have become almost comfortable offering sincere prayers

for peace, for healing, and for God's presence in patients' lives. I had thought that my own theology would get between us and turn those prayers into lies. But when I open my mouth, the particulars of my own beliefs become enormously unimportant. . . . When I am praying for a patient in the hospital, it's not about me. The prayer is theirs, and I am just the conduit for their deep need. Their prayers flow between us in those terrible moments of loss and diagnosis and anxiety, and I speak them into the world. Not for God to hear, as far as I am concerned, but for *us* to hear.

I never thought I could truly *pray*, because there's no one listening. But here, someone *is* listening. Those words of gratitude and love and hope are heard by those who most need to hear them. Heard by Ernesto, and his family, and by me. Those prayers are powerful, and those prayers were prayed by an atheist.

In light of the chaplain's testimony, we might say that the encounter with Ernesto's family mobilized her compassion and passion as a spiritual caregiver in a new and compelling way. She was able to connect with the family deeply and engage them spiritually on their terms—not hers. In her reflection on the nature and role of prayer in spiritual practice, she says:

> Christian prayer is different from Muslim prayer, is different from Buddhist prayer, is different from Jewish prayer. And I hadn't thought *atheist* prayer was a thing that could exist.
>
> But this, speaking aloud the prayer of another and lending my voice and the strength of my heart to the belief of someone who needs to feel their God listening, this I can do.[3] The prayer that I pray is an articulation of our connection, a deep investment in the lives and beliefs of fellow human beings. [Quoting Rabbi Abraham Joshua Heschel:] Prayer cannot bring water to parched land, nor mend a broken bridge, nor rebuild a ruined city; but prayer can water an arid soul, mend a broken heart, and rebuild a weakened will. . . . Sometimes, being in community is more important than being in agreement.
>
> I no longer run from prayer. I am learning something. Can an atheist pray, and why would she want to? After today, let the answers to these questions be a little less clear, and let us remember

---

3. Here and in this statement later in the excerpt are fine illustrations of *code-switching*: "To pray the prayers of others with our whole hearts, to stop trying, for half a breath, to make a prayer fit neatly into our theology . . ." In the context of spiritual caregiving, code-switching is using the languages, rituals, and practices of the care receivers as a hermeneutic-therapeutic, communicative tool. It is one of the strategies discussed in chapter 5 of this book.

how it can feel to pray the prayers of others with our whole hearts, to stop trying, for half a breath, to make a prayer fit neatly into our theology, and just let it come. To open ourselves up to some change, to pray heartily, and to learn something.

It is clear that the caregiving situation was transformational for the spiritual caregiver. Significantly, Chaplain Fritsche reports having experienced healing in several areas—enhanced vocational understanding, deepened "therapeutic love," and strengthened clinical competence. Such growth can be assessed and appreciated in light of a framework for desirable holistic competence as follows: academic-interdisciplinary ("knowing" competencies), personal-spiritual ("being" competencies), and professional-ministerial ("doing" competencies).[4] More simply put, Sally Fritsche became a better chaplain!

Evaluation

The account of the chaplain's caregiving encounter with Ernesto's family illustrates several key features of appropriate and effective spiritual care practice. For the care receivers, her praying was both psychologically functional and theologically appropriate;[5] it was fitting for the family's religious

---

4. Chapter 6 of this book has a thorough presentation of a competency profile following this framework, including pedagogies for the holistic formation of interfaith spiritual caregivers.

5. See Hunsinger, *Theology and Pastoral Counseling*, 130–50. As a pastoral theologian, Hunsinger proposes to work with a formal "Chalcedonian pattern" according to Karl Barth's theological legacy. In this light, the key to a fitting appropriation of psychological perspectives by pastoral counselors lies in the following three methodological conditions. First, they must respect the integrity of psychology as a human science in providing a distinct reading of the human situation, with the understanding that other readings, including that of theology, are possible and indeed necessary. Second, diverse readings must be kept side-by-side in our search for complementary insights and more complete knowledge. Finally, pastoral counselors must hold these disciplines in an asymmetrical relationship, maintaining the conceptual priority of theology over psychology. In other words, the contributions of psychology and psychotherapy must be subordinate to claims, frameworks, and perspectives grounded in the biblical-theological foundations of pastoral care and counseling. Those three conditions thus address key epistemological and methodological questions pertaining to the relationship between psychology and theology. See also Hunsinger, "Interdisciplinary Map."

For other models of conceptualizing interdisciplinary integration from a Christian perspective by psychologists, counselors, and psychotherapists in the United States, see Holeman, *Theology for Better Counseling*; Sandage and Brown, *Relational Integration*;

beliefs and spiritual practices. Put in terms of the psychology of religion and spirituality, the chaplain facilitated "positive religious coping."[6] The relationship co-created by caregiver and care receivers made it possible for those experiencing anticipatory grief to create meaning in the face of Ernesto's impending death, to garner emotional control, to acquire comfort from a sense of closeness to God, and to experience intimacy with each other.

All of these outcomes are indicators of what we might call healthy spirituality. Such a claim, however, calls for further discussion of the place and role of *interdisciplinary* views in psycho-spiritual assessment, as proposed below. In other words, more is needed than the spiritual assessment resources offered exclusively from a social science perspective.[7]

INTERDISCIPLINARY PERSPECTIVES ON PSYCHO-SPIRITUAL ASSESSMENT

One way of exploring the question of "healthy" and "toxic" spiritualities is to study them using an interdisciplinary approach that includes both psychological and theological norms, as suggested in the diagrams that follow. Readers should keep in mind that I write explicitly as a Christian practical theologian. My theory and practice of spiritual care always reflect my theological grounding, including its normative claims regarding the nature of reality and of human wholeness, health and healing, moral discernment, and related concerns.

Even when they do not identify with any religious tradition, as in Chaplain Fritsche's case, spiritual caregivers must competently address and respond to these and related questions—and some kind of normative

---

Entwistle, *Integrative Approaches;* and Callaway and Whitney, *Theology for Psychology and Counseling.*

For analogous efforts from representatives of other traditions, see Al-Karam, *Islamically Integrated Psychotherapy;* Isgandarova, *Islamic Spiritual and Religious Care;* Ali et al., *Mantle of Mercy;* Sanford, *Kalyanamitra;* Sutton et al., *Hindu Chaplaincy;* and Chander and Mosher, *Hindu Approaches.*

6. For more on "positive religious coping" and "negative religious coping," see Pargament, *Psychology of Religion and Coping.* For discussion of "spiritual coping to conserve the sacred" and "spiritual coping to transform the sacred," see Pargament, *Spiritually Integrated Psychotherapy,* 94–128. Chapter 4 of this book focuses on the question of religious and spiritual struggles and spiritual toxicity.

7. See Hodge, *Spiritual Assessment in Social Work.*

criteria will always be operative in our assessment and therapeutic approach, even as we spiritual caregivers seek not to impose our views on care receivers. And it is precisely in light of a certain theological grounding, such as a Christian one, that the outcome of the chaplain's care for Ernesto and his family can be assessed and considered "theologically adequate." With a Christian theology of the Holy Spirit, for example, I can interpret the chaplain's caregiving work as an event in which she became a partner not only with Ernesto's family but also with the Spirit of God—regardless of her desire for, or awareness of, such partnership. It is also possible that Ernesto's family experienced the chaplain as an instrument of divine grace in light of their Christian faith. And Chaplain Fritsche can, of course, also evaluate the caregiving event according to the normative guidelines of her Unitarian Universalist tradition.[8] In other words, whether or not care receivers and caregivers share a certain theological framework is not, in and of itself, a major factor in the interfaith spiritual caregiving relationship.[9]

---

8. The Unitarian Universalist (UU) tradition does not have a shared creed but nevertheless holds some fundamental assumptions and values that serve as a normative moral guide: The inherent worth and dignity of every person; justice, equity and compassion in human relations; acceptance of one another and encouragement to spiritual growth in the congregations; a free and responsible search for truth and meaning; the right of conscience and the use of the democratic process within congregations and in society at large; the goal of a world community with peace, liberty, and justice for all; respect for the interdependent web of all existence of which we are a part; promoting personal journeys toward spiritual wholeness by working to build a multicultural Beloved Community by actions that dismantle racism and other oppressions in UU people and institutions. Those principles are to be lived out within a living tradition of wisdom and spirituality drawn from sources as diverse as science, poetry, scripture, and personal experience. See Unitarian Universalist Association, *Bylaws and Rules*.

9. Empirical studies in the Netherlands demonstrate that the religious identity of the spiritual caregiver had no significant influence on the satisfaction of clients who received interfaith care from the spiritual caregivers. In other words, the clinical competence of the caregivers was of paramount importance regardless of the tradition they represented. See Liefbroer, *Interfaith Spiritual Care*, 117–48. The author concludes that "although religious and spiritual differences may play a role with regard to certain faith-specific roles and acts, in most spiritual care practices religious and spiritual differences with regard to spiritual caregivers' and clients' religious affiliation play a minor role" (221).

It should be noted that those empirical studies do not focus on or take into consideration the place and function that the caregivers' normative worldviews (theological or otherwise) also always play together with clinical competence narrowly understood. We can assume that the normative frameworks of those Dutch caregivers somehow facilitate, reinforce, or complement their clinical competence in interfaith situations. The contributors in Schipani, *Multifaith Views*, represent Aboriginal, Hindu, Buddhist, Jewish, Christian, Muslim, and Humanist traditions. All of them make explicit how their normative

Spiritual care providers must always be able to assess care receivers' spirituality and help them access their spiritual resources in the direction of healthy integration. To effectively do so, spiritual caregivers, and chaplains in particular, should learn to employ both *psychological* analyses and *theological* reflection (which can include non-theistic philosophical-ethical frameworks) of spirituality and "spiritual issues." An integration of these two kinds of analysis and reflection will inform the actual caregiving practice as well as an appraisal of the overall caregiving process, its goals, and its outcomes. In other words, theological literacy, fluency, and reflexivity are necessary features of competent spiritual care.[10]

Some theological (or philosophical-ethical) criteria and judgment—depending on the epistemological "weight" one gives to theology/philosophy/ethics—may even determine *a priori* that some spiritualities can never be "healthy" even if they are psychologically functional (e.g., fear reducing, anxiety neutralizing, integrating, etc.). In the diagram below, options 2^{11} and 4 may be considered psychologically functional but are, in my view, theologically inadequate. Conversely, theological norms may determine that certain spiritualities are "healthy" (or faithful, from a certain theological perspective) despite their possibility of being psychologically dysfunctional, as in options 5 and 7 in the diagram. From an

---

theological/philosophical sources inform, inspire, and guide their spiritual care theory and practice. Chapter 3 of this book discusses common ground and normative distinctness in interfaith spiritual care.

10. Doehring, *Practice of Pastoral Care*, 85–115. Doehring defines these terms as follows: "Theological literacy involves knowing about various theological perspectives or second-order ways of reflecting on religious and spiritual experiences. Fluency involves being able to use these perspectives in a fluid and embodied way in the practice of pastoral and spiritual care. Caregivers become fluent when they integrate and inhabit their intentional theology in the practice of pastoral and spiritual care.... Theological reflexivity involves tracking how one's personal theology (espoused and embodied) shapes a caregiving relationship. Pastoral and spiritual caregivers monitor how their embedded theologies are emotionally evoked under stress. They use their theological education to assess whether their personal theologies are life-giving or life-limiting in particular contexts of care. They are also accountable for drawing on their theological education to assess the care seeker's embedded and espoused beliefs, values, and practices. They draw on both their personal as well as public theologies to collaborate with care seekers in co-constructing life-giving contextual beliefs and values that can be tested in practice" (192).

11. For an interdisciplinary study of fundamentalism, see Schipani, "Fundamentalism as Toxic Spirituality," 178–207.

interdisciplinary perspective, only options 1 and 3 are both theologically adequate *and* psychologically functional—and therefore truly "healthy" spiritualities.

	theologically adequate	theologically inadequate
psychologically functional	1. life-giving, community-building spiritualities	2. spiritualities connected with "Prosperity Gospel" or with fundamentalism
	3. spiritualities that see the self-limiting Divine as a benevolent partner in one's suffering and in one's healing process; God is closely present with compassion, in solidarity Positive religious coping: emotional-spiritual comfort; strength, peace	4. spiritualities that see a micromanaging God as one who "knows better ... has a plan for my life ... is testing me .... I suffer here but will be compensated in heaven .... I've been chosen for this test" Positive religious coping: meaning and purpose clarified; "blessings in disguise"
psychologically dysfunctional	5. prophetic spirituality deemed antipatriotic by the government	6. spirituality of People's Temple that led to mass suicide
	7. spiritualities that see God as "just and wise, and has made us free .... We face the consequences of that freedom [accident, illness]" Negative religious coping: increased sense of vulnerability, weakness, diminished hope	8. spiritualities that see a micromanaging God as one who "is punishing me ... has abondoned me .... I'm not worthy of God's love" Negative religious coping: increased angst, guilt, isolation, despair

Illustration of an interdisciplinary assessment (1)

Applying psychological and theological norms (Hunsinger model) (1).

If I have successfully made a case for interdisciplinary competence, it follows that the present emphasis within the caregiving world on research-informed "best practices" and "outcome-driven" work should be connected with excellence in theological (or philosophical) reflection in all forms of pastoral and spiritual care. Indeed, competent interdisciplinary reflection can then be viewed as one of the indispensable "best practices" in the competency profile of spiritual caregivers.[12]

Application

Let us consider further the case of praying during a counseling session or a hospital visit, and we will assume that the patient either requested the prayer or gladly welcomed it when the spiritual care provider offered. Of course, there are many different ways of praying wisely for a care receiver, whether in a counseling setting or in a healthcare center. But we might safely say that in all instances, prayers, blessings, or words of support and guidance in the face of crisis should be sources of comfort or healing as they communicate some deep spiritual-theological truth (e.g., the sustaining presence of grace, however understood or defined, in all circumstances). At the same time, such prayer must be mentally and emotionally helpful (e.g., by fostering trust and hope in the face of anxiety and fear, by including the healthcare team and the family, etc.). Regretfully, there are also harmful ways of offering care, as suggested by cases 2, 3, and especially 4 in the diagram below.

---

12. The case studies in the collection edited by Fitchett and Nolan demonstrate competence in their *psychologically* informed spiritual assessment and *psychotherapeutically* informed caregiving approaches and interventions (e.g., by recognizing transference-countertransference in the caregiving relationship, by applying Acceptance and Commitment Therapy, etc.). *Theological* analysis and insight, however, are either undeveloped or absent in these essays. Pastoral theologians Todd, Anderson, and Cobb allude to that deficiency in their critical responses to the case studies included in the second volume. Says Cobb, "if theology is to remain a qualifying discipline for chaplains, then theological reflexivity should be a lively feature of chaplaincy case studies, both in terms of expounding a chaplain's working theology and generating new theological insights." Cobb, "Critical Response," 219.

In the case of pastoral counseling, Rogers-Vaughn has exposed the erosion of theological reflection in both training programs and counseling practice. In "Best Practices in Pastoral Counseling; Is Theology Necessary?", he connects the marginalization of theology to the dominance of Neoliberalism and the overarching free-market ideology and practices. Rogers-Vaughn, *Caring for Souls*.

See also Stone and Duke, *How to Think Theologically*; and Graham et al., *Theological Reflection*.

	theologically adequate	theologically inadequate
psychologically functional	1. prayer that elicits a sense of grace and activates emotional and spiritual resources of the patient and family	2. prayer that momentarily alleviates anxiety and fear by persuading one that quick healing is available
psychologically dysfunctional	3. prayer that focuses on human fragility or vulnerability, while failing to alleviate present anxiety	4. prayer that associates one's medical condition with God's judgment and condemnation

Illustration of an interdisciplinary assessment (2)

Applying psychological and theological norms (Hunsinger nodel) (2).

COMMON GROUND IN SPIRITUAL CARE

Literature on spiritual care across traditions and cultures allows us to identify a number of shared concerns regarding both its theory and practice—and multicultural and multifaith collegial conversation and collaboration can offer us something similar.[13] Common ground cannot be explained only in terms of caregivers' similar clinical training or formation, but rather as reflecting the reality of the holy ground of human encounter created in spiritual caregiving situations (as illustrated in our case study). Indeed, these encounters deal with fundamental needs and questions around transcultural and transreligious issues of meaning, connectedness, vocation, and mystery—in short, the essential concerns of the human spirit through the ages.

This phrase, the human spirit through the ages, implies a number of claims grounded in the basic assertion that *spiritual* cannot be separated from *psychological*.[14] First, we are human because we are spiritual beings; spirit is the essential dimension of being human. Second, we can understand

---

13. It is not primarily a question, however, of finding some common (minimum) denominator shared by everybody; distinctness and difference must also be duly recognized.

14. The next chapter offers a detailed proposal of one way of understanding "spirit" in pastoral and spiritual care.

spirituality as the ways in which our spirit searches or longs for, experiences ("inner" sense), and expresses ("outer" manifestations) certain interrelated aims: namely, *meaning* (truth seeking, wisdom, faith); *communion* (with others, nature, oneself, and the Divine); and *purpose* (or life orientation). Such a claim that meaning, communion, and purpose name fundamental, existential experiences and expressions of our human spirit is consistently confirmed by evidence-informed clinical work and supervision, comparative analysis of sacred texts, research in cultural anthropology, and comparative studies including literature in the fields of pastoral and spiritual care, and spiritual direction in particular.[15]

Another commonality—in addition to that of the human spirit and spirituality—is the central place and role of *wisdom* in diverse traditions. Wisdom can be basically understood both as a way of life and as discernment of the journey forward in the face of life challenges and struggles. That is, the shape of spiritual care is of a dialogical-hermeneutical process, one in which a normative body of existentially relevant knowledge "dialogues" with the contextually applicable resources of the people involved to discern a wise course of action.[16] In all cases, holistic formation of spiritual caregivers includes work on academic-interdisciplinary, personal-spiritual, and clinical-professional sets of competencies, as already mentioned.

CORE COMPETENCIES FOR SPIRITUAL CAREGIVERS

Two special core competencies, *bilingual proficiency* and a four-dimensional view, can be underlined at this point.[17] The unique contribution of spiritual caregivers—whether pastoral ministers, counselors, psychotherapists, chaplains, or others—is that they can view and work with the

---

15. See Mabry, *Spiritual Guidance Across Religions*.

16. For a reframing of pastoral counseling along these lines, see Schipani, *Way of Wisdom*. In this book, I argue that the biblically grounded Jewish-Christian wisdom tradition offers a way of doing practical theology that can help redefine the counseling process and its overarching goals.

Recent texts representing different theological traditions are similarly wisdom-focused. See Friedman and Yehuda, *Art of Jewish Pastoral Counseling*; Al-Karam, *Islamically Integrated Psychotherapy*; Isgandarova, *Islamic Spiritual and Religious Care*; Sanford, *Kalyanamitra*; Sutton et al., *Hindu Chaplaincy*; and Chander and Mosher, *Hindu Approaches*.

17. Chapter 6 in this book provides a thorough presentation of necessary competencies for interfaith spiritual caregivers.

care receivers holistically, both psychologically and spiritually. Therefore, spiritual caregivers need to develop the core competency of "bilingual proficiency," understanding the languages and resources of both psychology and spirituality/theology (or non-theological worldviews, as in the case of Humanism and Buddhism) and employing such understandings and resources in spiritual assessment and all other verbal and nonverbal (e.g., rituals) caregiving practices.[18]

The spiritual caregiver's main function is to connect persons in crisis to their spiritual resources and community. Given the plurality of sociocultural and religious variables at work, caregivers will normally encounter situations that present either commonality, complementarity, or contrast and even conflict with their own spiritual framework (as seen in the diagram below). Specific illustrations could include: A Protestant caregiver cares for a grieving Jewish family in the hospital; a Humanist female chaplain blesses the stillborn baby of a Christian couple; a Buddhist caregiver helps a young man in despair and unable to pray; a Muslim therapist counsels a Christian woman suffering depression; a Jewish chaplain offers a Jewish ritual (washing hands) to a non-Jewish grieving husband and son; a Unitarian Universalist chaplain, who is an atheist, prays with a Catholic family;[19] a "progressive" Christian counselor wrestles with the challenge of caring well for a "conservative" Christian couple.[20] In analyzing these and other interreligious spiritual caregiving encounters according to the three concentric circles of the diagram below, Dagmar Grefe categorizes the situations as follows: (a) "common (universal) human experience,"[21] in which the caregiver functions primarily as *companion*; (b) "interconnected spiritual practice," in which the caregiver functions as *representative of the sacred*; and

---

18. The call for "bilingual competence" also appears in other writings on chaplaincy. See Caperon et al., *Christian Theology of Chaplaincy*. Representing mainly Anglican voices in the United Kingdom, the text highlights a critical incarnational theology operationalized hermeneutically within the caregiving process as well as in reflection on the chaplaincy practice.

19. In our case study, the chaplain was able to care well as a *companion* and *representative of the sacred* for both caregiver and care receivers, and also as *resource agent* from her (the caregiver's) perspective. She could do so as a competent caregiver with, and because of, her Unitarian Universalist, all-inclusive normative philosophical-ethical grounding and framework.

20. "Intrafaith" caregiving situations, whether Christian or otherwise, may involve challenging manifestations of religious difference sometimes more difficult to navigate than those present in typical "interfaith" caregiving encounters.

21. For a thorough presentation of what is *universal*, *cultural*, and *unique* in caregiving theory and practice, see Augsburger, *Pastoral Counseling Across Cultures*, 48–78.

(c) "particular religious spiritual practice," in which the caregiver functions primarily as *resource agent* who relates (and often refers) care receivers and their families to their spiritual communities and resources.²²

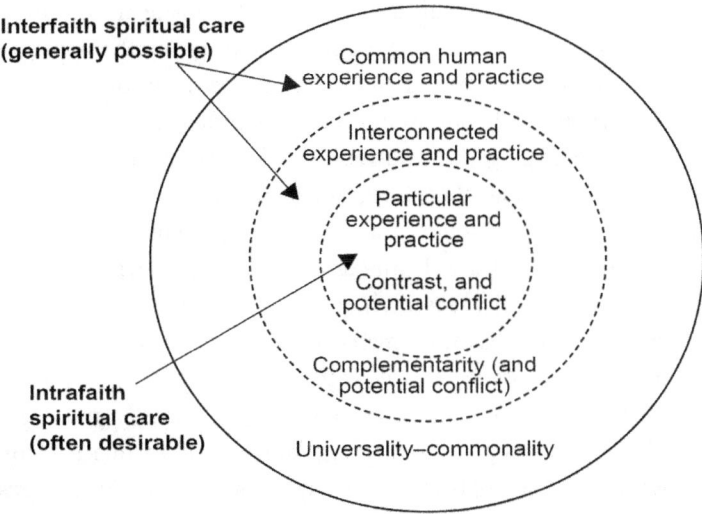

Three circles of spiritual care.

To sum up, in the face of diversity and difference, spiritual caregivers must be able to work with hermeneutical, communicative, and tradition-specific competence. And they must do so while self-reflexively acknowledging their own existential and religious location.²³ In all cases, competent

---

22. Grefe, *Encounters for Change*, 138–45. The diagram of three concentric circles comes from the work of the Sri Lankan theologian Wesley Ariarajah in connection with interfaith worship. He visualizes the possibility of interfaith worship as a public form of interreligious prayer with the use of analogous concentric circles. Ariarajah, *Not Without My Neighbor*, 49–53. Grefe was inspired by Ariarajah's model, as documented in her book.

23. Greider, "Religious Location and Counseling." This important essay alludes to three major forms of religious difference—interfaith, intrafaith, and difference due to religious multiplicity. It discusses challenges such as exacerbated power dynamics, implicit meanings and values rooted in religious locations, and professional competence and ethics challenged by differences in religious location. Greider highlights the central place of caregivers' self-differentiation and the key function of self-reflexivity. She also offers guidelines to facilitate connectedness in a therapeutic relationship: deliberate power-sharing, language care, and a modified, intentional presence characterized by humility, reverent curiosity, and gentle inquisitiveness. The essay ends on a hopeful note: "Our

spiritual caregivers will seek to engage care receivers in holistic care and on the care receivers' terms.

In addition to such bilingual proficiency, spiritual caregivers can also helpfully employ a four-dimensional view of reality. Psychotherapeutic and psychiatric approaches normally assume a two-dimensional view involving the self (or selves in the case of couples, family, or group therapy) and the lived world. The relatively recent and ongoing "recovery" of spirituality in healthcare, particularly in counseling and psychotherapy, also emphasizes assessing[24] and engaging the care receiver's beliefs and other sources of meaning and hope,[25] and then integrating spirituality into the therapeutic process,[26] including through practices such as meditation, prayer, and sacred readings.[27] This is a welcome development. However, much is still missing in terms of clinical research, theoretical reflection, and the actual caregiving practice. For example, many clinicians and theorists tend to collapse "spiritual" into "psychological" without recognizing their inseparable yet distinct manifestations.[28] Others, however, consistently and explicitly operate within psychological frameworks and norms[29] while recognizing the distinct contribution of theology. In any event, the relationship between

divergencies can impel us to search together for something *more*, perhaps something like wisdom" (17–53).

24. See Richards and Bergin, *Spiritual Strategy for Counseling*, 219–49; and Hodge, *Spiritual Assessment in Social Work*.

25. See Miller, *Integrating Spirituality*; Pargament, *Spiritually Integrated Psychotherapy*; and Pargament, *APA Handbook*.

26. For helpful illustration of the inclusion of resources aimed at engaging client's spirituality in therapy, see Aten and Leach, *Spirituality and the Therapeutic Process*. For a practical guide on how to engage clients spiritually, see Jones, *Spirit in Session*.

27. Plante, *Spiritual Practice in Psychotherapy*.

28. An important exception is Jones, *Spirit in Session*.

29. See Pargament and Exline, *Working with Spiritual Struggles*. After identifying the psychological orientation of the book, the authors state: "This psychology is not to be confused with theology. Psychology has nothing to offer when it comes to finding the 'ultimate truth,' but it can speak in volume to perceptions of truth and their effects in people's lives—the footprints left by faith . . . It means that we primarily use a *psychological lens* to view supernaturally focused beliefs and experiences" (21–22).

Pargament and Exline also acknowledge that assessing brokenness and wholeness, like in any other effort to help people, always involves highly value-laden evaluation as an essential part of the work of practitioners. "Some kind of evaluative frame of reference is needed to assess clients' strengths and weaknesses, identify reasonable goals for treatment, and determine progress toward growth of decline" (36). Strictly speaking, that is a reference to the necessary inclusion of axiological (and thus, meta-psychological) criteria stemming from religious, moral, or philosophical sources.

the psychological and the spiritual dimensions can be further understood in light of theological contributions such as the following two, summarized in the next three paragraphs.

Paul Tillich was a systematic theologian whose interests and contributions included the areas of psychology and health.[30] Key to understanding Tillich's theology is what he called the "method of correlation." Simply stated, it is an approach that connects insights from Christian revelation with fundamental issues raised by existential, psychological, and philosophical analysis.[31] Writing as a philosopher of being in his classic work, *The Courage to Be*, Tillich shows a way of distinguishing "pathological" and "existential" anxiety as matters of particular concern, respectively for psychotherapists and pastoral counselors or chaplains. For the latter, the existential (or spiritual) anxieties related to the threefold threat of nonbeing—meaninglessness, condemnation, and annihilation—are the special focus.[32] In Tillich's case, ontological categories thus become the bridge connecting theological and psychological constructs.

Practical theologian James E. Loder offers another framework for human reality that adds two more elements. For him, the four dimensions of human existence are the self, the lived world (environment), the Void (possibility of nonbeing), and the Holy (possibility of new being). "All four dimensions are essential," asserts Loder, "and none of them can be ignored without decisive loss to our understanding of what is essentially human."[33] In the third of these dimensions, the Void, human existence is destined to annihilation and the ultimate absence of being. The many faces of the Void include existential loneliness, despair, and death. But the fourth dimension, the Holy, has—by the power of the Spirit of God—the capacity to transform the other three dimensions.[34] An adaptation of the model follows below.

---

30. See Tillich, *Meaning of Health*.

31. That theological method of correlation was subsequently revised by Tracy and Browning. They proposed a more dynamic and dialectic interaction between theology and social sciences, and philosophy, as "mutually critical correlation." See Tracy, *Blessed Rage for Order*; and Browning, *Fundamental Practical Theology*.

Muslim psychotherapist and practical theologian Isgandarova articulates a correlation approach inspired in the contributions of Tillich, Tracy, and Browning, as a way of connecting Islamic theology with the social sciences. She does so, however, while affirming the primacy of her normative Islamic sources and framework. See Isgandarova, "Correlational Approach."

32. Tillich, *Courage to Be*, 32–77.

33. Loder, *Transforming Moment*, 69.

34. Loder, *Transforming Moment*, 80–91.

```
            The Sacred—offer of new being
      "abundant life" (wholeness, communion, meaning,
           hopefulness, freedom, purpose, destiny ....)

                      within the | contexts of
         persons     ------------|------------the lived world
                                 |   (nature and society-culture
                                 |        family, community)

            The Void—threat of non-being
   "languishing life" (emptiness, alienation, meaninglessness,
           despair, bondage, aimlessness, fate ....)
```

A four-dimensional framework for spiritual care.

When applied to Chaplain Fritsche's caregiving encounter with Ernesto and his Hispanic Catholic family, this model helps us to identify a number of spiritual and theological issues in addition to those normally accounted for within an exclusively psychological/social science framework. These could include a sense of mystery connected with images of God and divine will; the face of evil in ultimate separation and suffering; experience of divine presence and grace in the face of death; need for forgiveness and reconciliation related to unfinished business with the dying person; a deep bond between the biological family and the faith community as spiritual family; and grieving well while mobilizing internal and external spiritual resources.

It is important to realize that we can also analyze this caregiving encounter in terms of other normative worldviews and frameworks. For example, in the Unitarian Universalist tradition, chaplains' concern and reverence for the dignity and worth of every human being is a foundational principle for caregiving work. In their own words:

> Whether theist, deist, humanist, atheist, Christian, Jewish, Buddhist, or pagan, UU chaplains are engaged in the daily task of exploring the theological and philosophical constructs of *why and how we care* . . . I claim a theology that recognizes that truth flows from numerous sources, and that various religious paths can lead us toward a life of love and service. I believe that we are born and live as part of that creative, universal wholeness that is ultimately

unnamable yet that many call by the name of God. Because of circumstances that wound us or bad choices that we make, we often become blind to, or alienated from, the reality that the Holy is all around us and within us, sustaining and supporting us. My theology of spiritual care calls me to attempt to live daily with awareness of this holy reality . . . [and to] go into a patient's room . . . hoping to offer an 'I-thou' relationship that may be helpful for their physical or spiritual healing.[35]

Very likely, spiritual caregivers from diverse traditions could make the words of these Unitarian Universalist chaplains their own. If that is the case, the testimony with which this chapter ends can serve as a complement to the statement concerning necessary tasks in interfaith spiritual caregiving with which we started. The overview of the challenges and opportunities that we face today in different kinds of interfaith care situations will be expanded in the remainder of the book. The next chapter will further address the question of what is meant by *spirit* and *spiritual* in our discussion of spiritual care.

---

35. Hutt, *Call to Care*, xiii, 3. The first part of the quote comes from the editor's introduction, and the second part from Mauldin, "Inherent Worth and Dignity."

2

Engaging the *Spirit* in Spiritual Care

THE PURPOSE OF THIS CHAPTER, simply stated, is to offer a thorough, systematic response to the question, what is meant by *spirit* and *spiritual* in "spiritual care"? I remind the readers that I practice, teach, supervise, study, and reflect on spiritual care as a Christian man raised in a Latin American sociocultural context. My writing deliberately reflects understandings and convictions related to my social and religious locations and my professional-clinical practice. I assume that colleagues who represent other traditions and points of view will make helpful connections with their own frameworks, and I welcome them to offer meaningful criticism and suggestions.

Following my own story as a care receiver in the hospital, I discuss an understanding of being human with a tridimensional model applicable in spiritual care situations. A case study then serves as a clinical illustration for several theoretical issues to consider when relating mental health and spiritual health. The guidelines included for further reflection and practical integration arise out of my view of the unique contribution of spiritual care professionals—pastoral counselors and psychotherapists, chaplains and spiritual care specialists, and others—to health, healing, and wholeness.

HIGHLIGHTING SPIRIT: MY STORY AS A CARE RECEIVER

Early in the morning on Tuesday, May 20, 1997, I was taken to the emergency department of the local hospital with excruciating abdominal pain, and soon after arriving I underwent surgery for a ruptured appendix. Only two days before I had begun to feel some discomfort similar to the signs of a mild stomach flu, but the discomfort had become more intense as the hours progressed. (I have always had a low threshold for physical pain and, in retrospect, this may have contributed to saving my life.)

This was my first experience as a hospital patient, and when I woke up from surgery I naively assumed that my life was already almost back to "normal." Still under the effects of anesthesia, I began making work-related phone calls, but it did not take long for reality to set in. I realized I would need to adjust to the utterly disempowering effects of the hospital setting, and I also would face two difficult weeks of a painful and, at one point, uncertain recovery process.

Initially I was overwhelmed by the constant care I received on the part of several nurses, who dutifully and repeatedly checked my temperature and administered a number of procedures (including a well-intentioned yet unnecessary and painful catheter on the second night). I also was at first uncomfortable, to say the least, when needing to be washed by a soft-spoken, deeply caring African American aid, though she eventually became a trusted companion. Obviously I had not been prepared to experience such dislocation, vulnerability, and loss of privacy and sense of agency. To make matters worse, I had to cancel a family trip to the Caribbean, which included lecturing at a theological school. And I knew I also would miss my seminary's commissioning and commencement celebrations at the end of the academic year. In other words, my situation was a textbook case of a critical incident (unexpected surgery) triggering a multidimensional crisis.

The most critical point came ten days after surgery. A scan prescribed in the face of a stubborn infection and unresponsive digestive system (despite my long walks on the hospital's sixth floor) was inconclusive. My doctor told my wife and me that another surgery was a possibility. In an effort to avoid that option, he decided to fight the infection more aggressively, significantly increase I.V. nourishment, and lessen my pain by inserting a naso-gastric tube (quite another procedure!) to release a huge amount of accumulated liquid. Fortunately, my condition soon began steadily improving, and I was released fifteen days after entering the emergency room.

It is well known that crises are potential occasions for transformation; what is less well known is the connection between this transformation and spiritual care. My own hospital experience became a major transforming event for me, not only through the medical care I received but also competent and timely spiritual care. This care was offered in short visits by my pastor and a trusted colleague and included listening and encouraging words, scripture reading, prayer and blessing, and anointing with oil. I also knew that many people—family members, friends, and others in near and faraway places— were praying for me. In short, I received the spiritual care and support I needed for the mental, emotional, and spiritual realities that accompanied my medical condition. Although this care represented primarily one faith tradition, I am confident that skilled caregivers representing different faith traditions also would have been able to care for me in transformative ways—or would have sought to supplement their care with interventions and resources appropriate to my Christian faith. (My confidence regarding the value and effectiveness of such intervention is connected, of course, with my understanding of interfaith competence—and hermeneutical, communicative, and tradition-specific competence in particular—as discussed in the previous chapter.)

A miracle-like change happened in the course of this healing process—I actually became a model patient. It was a change that surprised me and those who know me well as an overactive, eager, impatient, and sometimes restless person. I learned to cooperate with the care team of nurses, aides, technicians, and physicians and even relaxed enough to serve some of them in return; two shared their own personal challenges and struggles with me and, toward the end of my stay, I was drawn to mediate a conflict between a nurse and a technician.

My hospital room (and the sixth floor where it was located) became a familiar, almost homey place. And in spite of the frequent interruptions mandated by current standards of hospital healthcare, the nights became an anticipated time for restful meditation and prayer. Surprisingly, the wishes "for a speedy recovery" in some of the many get-well cards I received somehow did not feel fitting, as I realized that the healing process underway would take time. I further came to know that such a process would involve my whole being—body, soul, and spirit.

Under the circumstances, I managed to accommodate to the situation remarkably well; inner and outer resources undoubtedly helped me to adapt to the realities of the hospital setting in psychologically healthy ways. But something deeper also was going on, which I later recognized as manifestations of what I call my spirit. I was experiencing a new sense of existential meaning and truth, a transcendent sense of love and communion with God and others near and far, and a sense of purposeful reorientation and destiny. I believe that a process of spiritual transformation undergirded my mental and emotional health and very likely contributed to the healing of my body as well. Anxiety and fear of death in the face of the unknown gave way to peace and joy truly beyond understanding. I left the hospital with a profound sense of grace and gratitude.

Reflection on my hospitalization experience has led me to endeavor to describe and explain a model of *spirit* as a fundamental dimension of being human. During the last few years, I have shared the content of that reflection with a number of colleagues internationally and have also included it in my writings.[1] The following section presents the latest version of this tridimensional anthropology.

ON BEING HUMAN: A TRIDIMENSIONAL ANTHROPOLOGY

I approach the question of what we mean by "being human" from the perspective of a theological anthropology grounded broadly in biblical literature and specifically in the New Testament writings of Paul the apostle. Even though one does not find a systematic anthropology in Paul's writings, his understanding of human nature can be drawn from pastoral and theological reflections he has contextually articulated in various epistles. I find it useful to critically reappropriate this Pauline legacy to address anthropological concerns raised in the discipline of pastoral theology and spiritual health and in the profession of spiritual care.[2] I trust that spiritual

---

1. Schipani, *Multifaith Views*, 149–66; and Schipani, "Pastoral and Spiritual Care."

2. The following observations are supported by Pauline scholarship (see Dunn, *Theology of Paul*, 51–78):
   - "Body" (*soma*) includes but is larger than physical body; it is a relational concept denoting the person embodied in a particular environment. "Body" for Paul expresses the character of created humankind—embodied existence—that makes possible a social dimension to life, that is, participation in human community. The concept is, for the most part, morally neutral. (In contrast, the notion of "flesh" [*sarx*] in the epistles, which is never equated with "body" [*soma*], is for the most part morally negative; it connotes human finitude, vulnerability, and proclivity to sinful behavior.)
   - "Soul" (*psyche*) denotes the person and the focus of human vitality. It includes the dimensions of "heart" (*kardia*, the seat of affection and will) and "mind" (*nous*, reason or rationality). By integrating Hebrew and Greek anthropological views, "Paul . . . sought . . . to maintain a balance between the rational, the emotional, and the volitional." Dunn, *Theology of Paul*, 75.
   - "Spirit" (*pneuma*) is that dimension of the human being by means of which the person can relate most directly to (the Spirit of) God. It is the deeper, transcendence-oriented or "God-ward" dimension of the human self. In fact, for Paul it is by opening the human spirit to the Holy Spirit that human beings can become truly whole and experience newness of life expressed interpersonally and communally with "spirit-fruit"—love, joy, peace, patience, kindness, generosity, faithfulness, gentleness, and self-control. Hence, the holistic blessing: "May the

care theorists and practitioners representing other traditions might find the following claims and observations meaningful in some ways, and I am open to being challenged and enriched by their views as well.[3]

Viewed from this Pauline-informed perspective, humans are embodied, psychosocial, and spiritual beings. A tridimensional anthropology of body, psyche, and spirit can thus be pictured structurally, as in the diagram that follows. The external full line symbolizes bodily separateness from others; the other two dotted lines represent the close connection between body and psyche (as appreciated from long ago, for instance, in so-called psychosomatic pathology and medicine), and even closer relationship between psyche and spirit. This view also implies that we are social beings embedded in family, community, and social systems (or "webs") and cultural contexts.

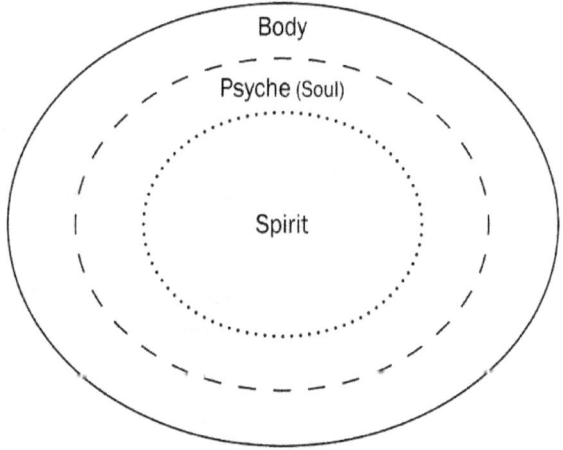

A tridimensional view (within family and social contexts).

The *psychological* and the *spiritual* dimension are integrated and inseparable—yet they are also distinct and distinguishable. Psychotherapist Russell Siler Jones says it well: "The body-rootedness of 'spirituality' and 'religion' reminds us that spirit is inseparable from body. But spirit is also inseparable from 'psyche' and from the relational and social fabric of our

---

God of peace [Godself] sanctify you entirely; and may your spirit and soul and body be kept sound and blameless . . ." (1 Thess 5:23).

3. See Olson, *Religious Theories of Personality*. In this text, representatives of Hinduism, Buddhism, Taoism, Judaism, Christianity, and Islam offer contributions regarding human nature, personality development, psychopathology, therapeutic change, and clinical practice.

lives ... A spiritual experience is also a physical experience, a psychological experience, and a social experience."[4] Among his clinical observations on this subject that resonate with those presented in this chapter: that the spiritual dimension is integrated and interwoven with all the other dimensions of human experience (mind, body, relationships, and more); that the spiritual dimension is always present, affecting caregivers' health and well-being for better or worse; that implicit spiritual experiences occur at the fuzzy intersection of the psychological and the spiritual; and that explicit and implicit spiritual experiences are always a resource to draw upon in helping people stabilize, change, and heal.[5]

Thinking about the *psyche*, at least since Aristotle, has largely conceptualized its manifestations in terms of thinking and knowing (*cognition*), feeling and relating (*affection*), and choosing and acting (*conation, volition*). Contemporary psychology refers to those closely interrelated expressions of the psychological self as cognitive, affective, and volitional *registers of behavior*. All key psychological constructs—e.g., *intelligence* (whether viewed traditionally or as emotional, social, or moral intelligence) and *personality*—are usually reflected and studied in terms of cognitive, affective, and volitional behaviors. Analogously in the case of pathologies, mental and emotional disorders can be broadly defined as health conditions characterized by alterations of thinking, mood, or behavior (or some combination thereof) associated with distress and/or impaired functioning.

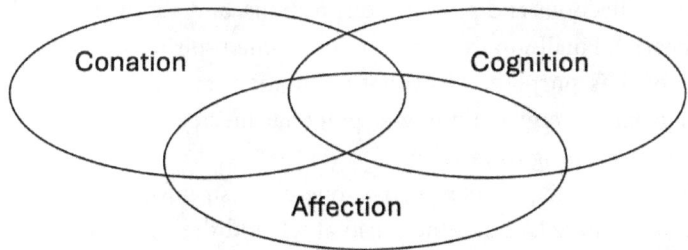

Threefold expression of the psyche.

I have proposed that the *spiritual dimension* can be visualized analogously as having interrelated expressions that I name *vision, virtue,* and *vocation*. Thus, the following drawing may be viewed as a functional model of the wholesome human spirit.

4. Jones, *Spirit in Session*, 37.
5. Jones, *Spirit in Session*, 9, 40.

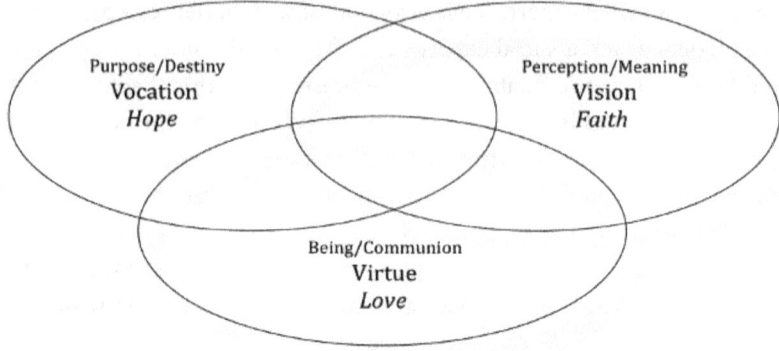

Threefold expression of a (wholesome) spirit.

Vision connotes ways of seeing and knowing reality—both that of the self and the world. Fundamentally, it names the need and potential for deep perception and meaning. Growth in vision necessitates deepening dispositions and behaviors such as heightened awareness, attentiveness, admiration and contemplation, critical thinking, creative imagination, and moral and spiritual discernment. *Virtue* connotes ways of being and loving; fundamentally, it is existential connectedness or being in communion, grounded in love and community. Growth in virtue may be viewed as requiring a process of formation and transformation that reshapes one's innermost affections and passions, dispositions, and attitudes (i.e., "habits of the heart"). Finally, in this model of the human spirit, *vocation* connotes a sense of life's purpose, existential orientation, and destiny. It is about investing one's energies, time, and potential in creative, life-giving, and community-building ways.[6]

From a theological perspective, one can also posit a direct connection between these facets of the spiritual self and the virtues of faith, love, and hope. Over the last several years, I have enjoyed significant dialogue and collaboration with caregivers from other traditions, including various kinds of humanism. These experiences suggest that they also can broadly consider the (religious and nonreligious) categories of faith, love, and hope as potentially helpful to name main sets of existential experiences or conditions concerning spirit (or the "spiritual dimension") and spirituality.

6. This model relates to Trinitarian anthropological conceptions throughout the history of Christian thought, all the way from Augustine, *Treatise on the Holy Trinity*, to LaCugna, *God for Us*.

Interestingly, from a psychological-developmental perspective, Erik Erikson established years ago a direct connection between "*hope, fidelity,* and *care* as the human strengths or ego qualities emerging from such strategic stages as infancy, adolescence, and adulthood . . . [and] such major creedal values ['highest spiritual aspirations'] as *hope, fidelity,* and *charity*." Erikson concluded that "it would be most instructive to pursue such parallels in different traditions and languages."[7]

In light of these observations, existential threats to the human spirit and spiritual health may include, respectively but not exclusively, manifestations such as the following: meaninglessness, emptiness, illusion, and deceit (deficiency in *vision* or *faith*); alienation, isolation, condemnation, and annihilation (deficiency in *virtue* or *love*); and aimlessness, disorientation/lostness, and despair (deficiency in *vocation* or *hope*). These and related existential threats can be considered as faces of the *void*—diverse spiritual struggles and/or expressions of a "languishing life" (as opposed to "flourishing life")—as presented in the previous chapter within the four-dimensional view of reality for spiritual caregivers. It is also possible to find helpful correlations between normal and pathological anxieties on the one hand, and existential (or spiritual) anxieties on the other hand, as also discussed in the first chapter.

In order to illumine this discussion further, let us consider now the situation of someone needing holistic care. It is an abbreviated and simplified case study based on a real-life counseling situation that I encountered.

CARING FOR ARTHUR

Arthur[8] was a seventy-eight-year-old man, born and raised in the Caribbean Islands, who had been in the United States for about thirty years. His wife had died three years earlier, after a painful dying process; his daughter and her family lived not far from him in the same town; and his son lived in another state. At the time I met Arthur he had a growing, inoperable tumor

---

7. Erikson, *Life Cycle Completed*, 58. Pastoral theologian Donald Capps draws on Erikson's life cycle theory, biblical narratives, and the Beatitudes to advocate for confronting "deadly sins" through cultivating "saving virtues." Capps, *Deadly Sins and Saving Virtues*. He further develops and reframes Erikson's theory in *Decades of Life*.

8. "Arthur" is the fictional name of a real care receiver for whom I changed several pieces of information concerning this experience of care to preserve confidentiality. I am grateful to him and hundreds of other care receivers like him with whom I have explored the inseparable and complex connection between mental and spiritual health.

increasingly compromising his digestive system, and hospice care was soon to be arranged for him. Arthur was referred to me by his family physician because he frequently experienced anxiety and depression. The diagnosis registered in Arthur's clinical chart was "adjustment disorder with mixed anxiety and depressed mood (309.28)."[9] He would continue using prescribed medication to lessen both his anxiety and depression and to manage pain.

Arthur and I established good rapport. He was eager to receive help, especially from someone who he thought might consider addressing his spiritual anguish, so he readily welcomed my therapeutic companionship. Arthur's personal and family story was seemingly unremarkable at first. However, as our relationship unfolded, he shared the secret of living with the burden of, in his words, unforgivable sin. He was struggling with guilt and the sense of having lost forever the opportunity to communicate regret to his wife and to receive forgiveness for not being more fully present with her during the last months of her life. He didn't feel free to talk with his children about the situation, and prayers of confession had not been helpful. The diagnosis of terminal illness compounded Arthur's sense of being in a truly limited situation and facing condemnation.

The goals and commitments that I set for myself in this situation as a spiritual caregiver are as follows.[10] First, I would accept Arthur's welcoming me and, in turn, welcome him into a safe and caring space where he could express himself freely. Second, I would represent and mediate Grace and Wisdom and a healing community for Arthur to move away from the severe disorientation linked to both his terminal illness and unresolved guilt and grief. Third, I would become, for a short while, a companion in Arthur's journey toward reorientation and, hopefully, healing even without physical cure (by being a witness who listens well, comforts him, helps him to embrace new life, guides him in a discernment process, and gently holds him accountable). And fourth, I would offer care and counseling competently—in this case, by deliberately employing a narrative approach as well as cognitive restructuring[11] to help Arthur re-story his life and to perceive his world more realisti-

---

9. American Psychiatric Association, *DSM-5*, 286–87.

10. It is essential for caregivers to have clarity regarding certain key goals and commitments that we must in principle set for ourselves and for which we are primarily responsible, even as we remain open to including appropriate expectations set by those for whom we care.

11. As a therapeutic intervention, cognitive restructuring is a broadly used method associated with cognitive psychotherapies. It is employed to help people change their learned negative cognitions and to teach them more realistic sets of beliefs, including the

cally, changing the misconceptions and expectations directly connected with his anxiety and depression.

Arthur and I agreed that our relationship would be oriented toward the following interrelated objectives: understanding what was actually going on in his life; revisiting his life story and spiritual journey with an eye to rekindling hope; finding specific, practical ways for him to transform the struggle with guilt and a sense of sinfulness while experiencing a closer communion with God; and making key decisions about next steps, especially regarding the transition to hospice care and the relationship with his family. In short, we were aiming to move from barely coping to an experience of healing and wholeness.

I sought a holistic approach to Arthur's medical care by engaging him psychologically and spiritually. The following sections present several key principles that undergirded my therapeutic relationship with him and continue to orient my views and practice of spiritual care. For now, let us consider the question of what is meant by *spiritual* in "spiritual care" by relating mental-emotional health and spiritual health. Such a theoretical exercise must include a number of interrelated considerations, as discussed below.

CONNECTING MENTAL HEALTH[12] AND SPIRITUAL HEALTH: UNDERSTANDINGS AND GUIDELINES FOR SPIRITUAL HEALTHCARE PRACTITIONERS[13]

The purpose of the following sections is twofold: to highlight issues encountered when relating current notions of mental health and spiritual health, and to suggest guidelines for further theoretical reflection and practical integration. The case of caring for Arthur will illustrate the kind of

---

practice of reformulating irrational thoughts in light of a new vision of reality.

12. I will use "mental health" and "mental and emotional health" interchangeably for the remainder of this chapter.

13. The group of "spiritual healthcare practitioners" includes pastoral counselors and psychotherapists, chaplains (a term increasingly reserved for caregivers who represent a certain faith tradition and/or who work in a faith-based healthcare institution), and "spiritual care and counseling specialists." This last group is defined by the Canadian Association for Spiritual Care as clinical practitioners who help people draw upon their own spiritual, religious, and cultural resources for direction, strength, wisdom, and healing as they journey through life's stages. "Competencies of CASC/ACSS Certified Professionals."

opportunity and responsibility that spiritual caregivers assume as they seek to care in a holistic manner.

THEORETICAL ISSUES FOR REFLECTION

Choosing Labels: Semantic Considerations

We can start by recalling that the word *health* is related etymologically to the Anglo-Saxon word from which *healing, holiness,* and *wholeness* are derived.[14] This is something to keep in mind as we consider the main senses of "mental health" and "spiritual health."[15] Those notions of "health" carry diverse meanings and connotations, including the following.

Mental or emotional health can be characterized simply as the capacity to think, feel, and behave in ways that enhance our ability to enjoy life and deal with the challenges and struggles we face.[16] Healthy and "mature" spirituality is harder to define. A safe but incomplete place to start is by looking for enduring and life-giving manifestations of meaning, purpose, peace, joy, love of self and others, connectedness with a transcendent source of light and grace and with the non-human environment, and so on.[17] Further, concepts of mental/emotional and spiritual "maturity" are often closely associated with mental and spiritual health (or "healthy spirituality"), especially in the case of adults. But are these terms really synonymous? It is helpful, therefore, to agree on some definitions or at least commonly held understandings for each of those concepts.

---

14. The World Health Organization defines health as "a state of complete physical, mental and social wellbeing and not merely the absence of disease or infirmity."

15. "Mental health" denotes not only a human condition that can be described and assessed somehow, but also a special kind of science or discipline, and a profession as well. The same can be said regarding "spiritual health." Our discussion of the relationship between mental and spiritual health can be enhanced by keeping in mind those three different kinds of meanings and connotations—a human condition, a science, and a profession—and their interrelationships.

16. Mental and emotional are often used as synonyms when discussing health and illness or "disorder" both colloquially and in academic or professional speech.

17. From a Christian perspective, "spiritual health" can be assessed, for example, by focusing on someone's relationship with God, others, oneself, systems and structures, and creation. Schrock, *Spiritual Health Inventory*. It is, of course, possible to identify a plurality of "healthy" spiritualities with distinct features, such as contemplative, prophetic, charismatic, etc. And it is also possible to assess unhealthy or "toxic" spiritualities, Christian or otherwise. Descriptions of healthy spirituality from diverse religious traditions can be found in Mabry, *Spiritual Guidance Across Religions*.

Another semantic point on which there is confusion, or at least inconsistency, is regarding the use of terms such as *soul* (in Greek, ψυχή/*psyche*) and *spirit* (πνεῦμα/*pneuma*). Such inconsistency is detectable both in everyday speech and in fields such as literature, philosophy, religious studies, and theology. I hold that it is helpful to assume a conceptual distinction between "soul" and "spirit," while maintaining their integration and inseparability within the larger, "tridimensional" understanding of being human.

Behind the Labels: Philosophical-Sociocultural-Theological Issues to Ponder

Our agenda for reflection and discussion must include a second set of issues that are not inherently *scientific*, strictly speaking; they are regarding the metaphysical and ethical non-neutrality of theoreticians and practitioners in the fields of both "mental" and "spiritual" health. "Mental health" and "spiritual health" are, in the language of philosophy of science, *practical human sciences;* in other words, not unlike education, those sciences deal with guidance, support, and transformation of human behavior and life. Therefore, they must develop goals and methodologies consistent with fundamental questions and norms of humanness, healing, and wholeness that stem in part from philosophical, theological, and other sources outside their respective scientific fields, narrowly viewed. The very notions of mental and spiritual "health" (and "maturity") rest on value-laden criteria. Those criteria are always articulated within specific sociocultural contexts (not normally recognized as such) and do change over time. For example, changing definitions and (psychopathological) criteria are easily documentable in the case of mental health,[18] as registered, for instance, in the history of the American Psychiatric Association's widely used *Diagnostic and Statistical Manual of Mental Disorders* (*DSM*). Further, in the case of both psychiatry and clinical psychology (including disciplines such as personality theory,

---

18. There is a reason for this significant difference between the histories of "mental health" and "spiritual health," including the fact that changing definitions and criteria for the latter are not easy to document. In any event, the discipline of spiritual health has always dealt with perennial questions concerning human life and the spirit, meaning and love, vocation and destiny, health, suffering, sickness and death, the divine, and so on. That is why we still benefit from appropriating the wisdom of ancient texts, for example. The field of mental health is much younger as a branch of modern medicine.

psychopathology, and psychotherapy theory) there exists a variety of views and approaches not necessarily compatible among themselves.[19]

Our reflection must always include explicit consideration of multicultural and multifaith factors that condition the very notions of "good" mental and spiritual health. Those factors also determine the approaches, methods, and treatments employed to support, enhance, or restore "health"—or to foster the experience of suffering and dying well—for the care receivers and their communities.

Authority and Power to Label: Ideological and Professional-Political Considerations

Related questions of ideology and power must also be part of this conversation. It matters greatly who has the authority and power to define "health" and to label "disorder," "sickness," and "cure." It matters also what kinds of assumptions and understandings determine the form and content of the definitions and labels, and the implications regarding care deemed appropriate in light of such categorizations. The following sets of issues immediately come to mind.

The challenge to consider ideological and professional-political factors obviously pertains to the field of mental health, especially considering the major role of powerful organizations such as the American Psychiatric Association.[20] It also relates to government and institutional entities that decide, for example, who qualifies to receive certain kinds of medical or psychological assistance, for how long, and under what conditions. Economic and financial considerations are, therefore, of great significance—whether or not we are dealing with public or private healthcare programs and centers, insurance policies, and related matters.

---

19. There are hundreds of clinical psychotherapeutic strategies roughly identifiable in terms of "families" of psychodynamic, behavioral, humanistic-existential, and systemic views and approaches. Spiritual caregivers can benefit greatly from their contributions, especially when their implicit metaphysical and ethical assumptions are duly unveiled and taken into consideration.

20. Psychiatrists, clinical psychologists, clinical social workers, and pastoral psychotherapists in the United States routinely use psychiatric labeling (or "diagnoses"). Potential conflict emerges to the extent that ethical and legal questions are raised (e.g., whether making diagnoses of mental illness constitutes a "medical" act requiring medical supervision, or whether insurance policies will pay for certain counseling or psychotherapeutic treatments, etc.).

We must also ponder ideological, legal, and other issues in the science and practice of spiritual health. Spiritual care providers need to work with normative understandings of "healthy" and "unhealthy" or "toxic" spirituality, which are heavily conditioned by one's ideological framework and its preferred approaches to care. This is an area where other sources can and must complement and, in some areas, revise and transform contributions of "classic" counseling and psychotherapeutic approaches. In my view, input from Positive Psychology, Gestalt Pastoral Care, feminist/eco-feminist, liberationist, and postcolonial psychologies, and pastoral theologies, is indispensable.

GUIDELINES FOR FURTHER REFLECTION AND PRACTICAL INTEGRATION

I sought to care for Arthur through the lens of my tridimensional view of spirit. I endeavored to assist him in a process of gaining wisdom in the sense of spiritual-moral intelligence—that is, wisdom demonstrated in improving discernment, making life-giving choices, and dying well. From this perspective, the overarching purpose of spiritual care included helping Arthur find new and better ways of seeing and understanding reality, and especially himself and others. (With restored vision, he would see better, as with the eyes of a caring and sustaining Divine). This would allow Arthur to find and create meaning in transforming ways. Second, our brief relationship would encourage Arthur to reappropriate the experience of personal integrity and having loved and been loved deeply. (With greater virtue, his heart would become restored to the heart of a reconciling and healing Divine). Third, spiritual healing also would entail a retrospective vocational reappraisal together with a fresh sense of ultimate purpose and destiny. (With renewed vocation, Arthur would experience a new realization of participating—in this life and somehow beyond it—in the life of the liberating and empowering Divine).

CONNECTING MENTAL AND SPIRITUAL HEALTH: INTRAPERSONAL DYNAMICS

As asserted above, psychological and spiritual dimensions can be viewed as distinguishable as well as integrated and inseparable. The following related claims are therefore in order. They are assumed to be relevant across diverse traditions and cultures.

In principle, the condition of mental health, emotional maturity, and wellness makes it possible to experience spirituality more freely (less fearfully, compulsively, or obsessively) and to express it more authentically than in the case of mental illness. Mental disorders and emotional immaturity always affect the subjective experience as well as the visible expressions of spirituality and spiritual health to some degree.[21] We must add, however, that mental health and emotional maturity are necessary but not sufficient conditions for spiritual health and maturity. Progress in the treatment of mental health does not automatically enhance people's spirituality and spiritual health; the spirit (or spiritual dimension) must be engaged intentionally.[22]

For instance, toxic spirituality in the form of sternly judgmental religiosity can seriously undermine mental health.[23] And spiritual healing, or *inner healing*, by the experience of grace and forgiveness, for example, always positively correlates with improvement in psychological health indicators. Therefore, even when spiritual caregivers are not mental health professionals strictly speaking, their work always engages care receivers psychologically in ways that can contribute significantly to improved mental health and emotional maturity.

Intrapersonal dynamics were clearly apparent in caring for Arthur. His mental and emotional distress, expressed with high levels of anxiety and depression, was directly related to unresolved grief and guilt, a weakened spirituality, and the painful realities of terminal physical illness. Arthur's psychological distress significantly affected his spiritual self; in turn, spiritual and

---

21. See Scazzero, *Emotionally Healthy Spirituality*; and Benner, *Soulful Spirituality*.

22. This claim is analogous to the possible connection between "natural" psychosocial development and spiritual (including moral) development in the course of our life cycle. The fact that psychological development occurs in the natural flow of our life does not ensure that spiritual and moral growth will take place as well. Nevertheless, such psychological development has the effect of opening broader and more complicated worlds to us, thus increasing the range and complexity of our spirituality. Hence, the range and complexity of our spirituality (e.g., in terms of deeper awareness of one's existential situation, sense of life orientation, connectedness with others, transcendence, etc.) and ways to nurture it (e.g., contemplation, meditation, prayer, compassionate service, etc.) tend to increase as well. Development can thus bring with it enhanced intentionality in, and responsibility for, both the intrapersonal ("inner") experience of spirituality as well as its visible ("outer") expressions or manifestations.

23. See Griffith, *Religion That Heals*.

moral anguish exacerbated Arthur's mental and emotional distress and, very likely, also made his struggle with cancer more difficult and painful. Arthur and I both hoped that spiritual care would help not only to restore spiritual health but also to alleviate this distress, while also bringing a measure of relief for his failing body.

As already asserted in the previous chapter, the unique contribution of all spiritual caregivers, whether counselors, psychotherapists, or chaplains, must be to view and work with care receivers holistically—engaging them psychologically as well as spiritually,[24] as suggested in the diagram that follows.

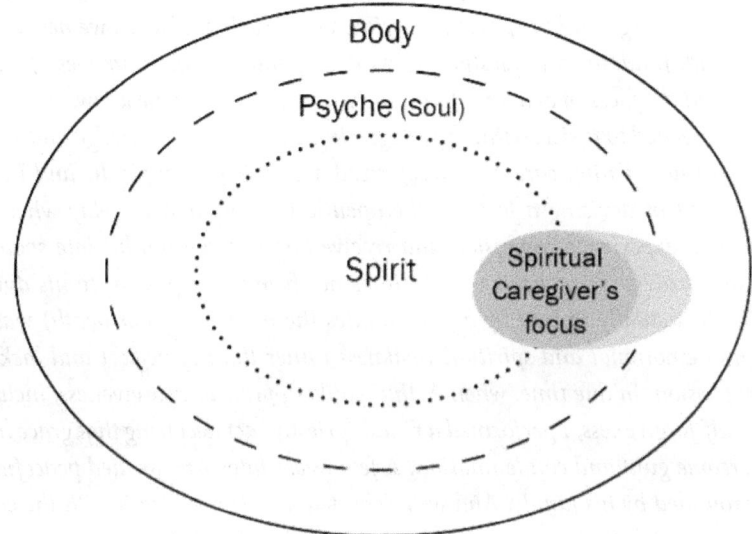

Spiritual care as holistic care.

SPIRITUAL CARE AS HOLISTIC CARE

Arthur was entering the final phase of his life journey. His three-year widowhood had been extremely challenging—and much more so since the diagnosis

---

24. This assertion does not imply that concern for and engagement with care receivers' bodies is absent. Even when the body as such is not the deliberate focus of spiritual caregiving practice, competent caregivers are always sensitive to body language and nonverbal communication. Further, they know when and how to suggest specific bodily activities such as breathing exercises, body posture and relaxation techniques, healing massage, etc. See Norberg, *Consenting to Grace*.

and treatment of cancer. He was a resourceful person who was able to take care of himself, but he had chosen to carry the burden of grief and guilt alone as a kind of shameful, self-inflicted punishment. Good relationships with children and grandchildren, a few friends, and occasional participation in worship services were necessary but insufficient resources at his disposal. At that particular juncture, spiritual healthcare became available for Arthur through the caregiving relationship with me, and he welcomed it.

Our caregiving relationship identified a number of issues to consider on a psychosocial level: a review of decisions that remained to be made regarding finances and personal belongings; anticipated personal and interpersonal adjustments connected with hospice care; and expectations and fears related to declining energy and the process of dying. On the spiritual level, we needed to deal with fundamental questions of guilt, sin, and sinfulness; images of God, fate, and the faces of evil; and forgiveness and grace, to name a few.

I needed to assist Arthur by integrating the kinds of knowledge and skills that define spiritual care as characterized above. For example, he and I collaborated in devising a form of therapeutic imaging and roleplay whereby he could experience confession and receive forgiveness from his late spouse. In this process we realized that Arthur's not being fully present to his dying wife (he actually missed by a few minutes the moment of her death) was a sign of emotional and spiritual weakness rather than of neglect and lack of compassion. In due time, when Arthur could appropriate forgiveness, including self-forgiveness, I performed a ritual "priestly" act declaring that grace had overcome guilt and condemnation. A few weeks later Arthur died peacefully, surrounded by his family. And we celebrated his life and death with the conviction that faith, love, and hope had ultimately prevailed.

RECAPITULATION: MANY FAITHS, ONE HUMAN SPIRIT

Simply stated, we are humans because we are spiritual beings. The spirit is an essential dimension of being human; hence the Judeo-Christian claim about our being created in God's image according to the words of Gen 1:26–27. So, in terms of the model sketched in this chapter, spirituality can be understood as the ways in which our spirit manifests itself through searching for, experiencing ("inner" sensations), and expressing ("outer" manifestations) *meaning* (truth, wisdom, faith); *communion* with others, nature, the divine, and oneself; and *purpose* or life orientation. As reported in the previous chapter, the claim that these dimensions of spirituality—meaning, communion, and purpose—name fundamental experiences and expressions of our human spirit is based on consistent and converging confirmation stemming from various sources. Among these are evidence-based clinical work and supervision, study and comparative analysis of sacred texts across traditions, contributions from cultural anthropology, intercultural and interfaith case studies, and literature in the fields of pastoral and spiritual care, and spiritual direction in particular. Once again, it should be clear that the construct of *spirit* is inseparable from that of *psyche;* so, the spiritual dimensions related to "longing" or "searching for" are viewed in continuity with ongoing psychic process and content.

The heuristic potential of this model of the human spirit and spirituality has also been tested beyond care and counseling, strictly speaking. For example, it has been applied to research on the structure and dynamics of religious fundamentalism from a spiritual health science perspective. Its toxicity can thus be assessed across cultures and traditions in terms of the threefold collapse that characterizes religious and other fundamentalisms as closed systems: collapse of meaning into dogmatism, a caricature of faith (epistemological failure); collapse of communion into sectarianism, a caricature of love (ethical failure); and collapse of purpose into proselytism/realized utopia, a caricature of hope (political failure).[25]

With those notions in mind, it is helpful to identify a wide variety of religious and non-religious spiritualities, including diverse streams within a given tradition. In the case of the Christian tradition, we can see a plurality of spiritualities such as contemplative, holiness, charismatic, social justice, evangelical, and incarnational.[26] Similarly, diverse spiritualities can be recognized within other religious traditions.[27] And analogous manifestations of spiritual toxicity can also be identified across cultures and religious traditions, as will be discussed later in this book.

Pastoral theologian Carrie Doehring's views of spirituality can be connected with the main claims presented in this chapter as an embodied and relational search for meaning and purpose in life, and a way of coping and connecting with a sense of transcendence or the sacred.[28] Doehring's

---

25. Schipani, "Fundamentalism as Toxic Spirituality." Material from that essay, as an analysis of fundamentalism across religious traditions, is included in chapter 4 of this book.

26. Foster, *Streams of Living Water*.

27. Mabry, *Spiritual Guidance Across Religions*.

28. Doehring, *Practice of Pastoral Care*, 19.

postmodern approach includes the description of "spiritual integration" with three components of spiritual orienting systems—ultimate beliefs, core values, and spiritual practices. She further highlights criteria for assessing whether specific spiritual orienting systems are life-giving or life-limiting. Doehring also demonstrates the importance of an intercultural and interreligious understanding, particularly in caring and reflecting upon traumatic situations. Her pastoral care approach can be adapted and applied in diverse social contexts while also attending to pre-modern, modern, and postmodern languages and epistemologies.[29]

The proposal offered in this book makes explicit the assumption of the transcultural or universal, non-culturally specific nature of the human spirit. As insightfully discussed by David W. Augsburger, this notion belongs in a category where "every human person is, in certain aspects, like all others."[30] The explicit anthropological claim is that, considered at their core, human beings demonstrate, contextually and particularly, the need and potential for meaning, communion, and purpose. At the same time, it is imperative to recognize that the spirit manifests itself uniquely within specific sociocultural contexts and faith traditions—"every human person is, in certain respects, like some others . . . and like no other."[31] Further, we keep in mind that the spirit is always engaged in an ongoing, dynamic process.

The universal manifestations of the human spirit have been compared to the melody of a song, and its diverse cultural and personal expressions to the many different lyrics associated with that very song. The Canadian National Anthem—"Oh Canada!" / "O Canada!"—offers a helpful analogy, according to spiritual care chaplain Patricia Driedger. The anthem is sung in English-speaking Canada, French-speaking Canada, and in the territory of Nunavut ("Uu Kanata!"): three different languages, three distinct meanings, but only one country and only one tune. Likewise, it is a common melody (paradigm of faith) rather than common lyrics (the specific tenets of faith themselves) that creates a foundation for multifaith spiritual care. In Driedger's own words:

> The shared melody of all spiritual traditions is heard in the questions of meaning and purpose. . . . The music of the spirit is expressed in the universal quest for love, inner peace, belonging, and

---

29. Doehring, *Practice of Pastoral Care*, 192.
30. Augsburger, *Pastoral Counseling Across Cultures*, 48–78.
31. Augsburger, *Pastoral Counseling Across Cultures*, 49.

> hope.... The role of the spiritual caregiver is to recognize the importance of the spiritual process in shaping all aspects of life and to provide accompaniment for people as they engage in the process... to help them become more aware of the ways in which their own framework of questions and answers impacts their health and their health-related choices.... They have to hone their skills in enabling the spiritual process without prescribing the spiritual content.... It is important that the caregiver be rooted in his or her own faith tradition because that rootedness enables the caregiver to understand the significance of the spiritual process.[32]

In a nutshell, the human spirit longs for wisdom in its search for meaning, communion, and purpose; and wisdom traditions address that search across cultures. At its best, all forms of spiritual care connect wisdom traditions with the longings of the human spirit in socioculturally and otherwise contextually pertinent ways. The next chapter expands the consideration of common ground among traditions, focused on the assumed universality of the human spirit discussed so far. It does so by highlighting the caring function of religious communities across cultures, and the central place of wisdom in spiritual care present in many theological traditions.

---

32. Driedger, "Different Lyrics," 132.

3

Common Ground

Community, Wisdom, and Discernment

THE MEMBERS OF INTERNATIONAL organizations such as the Society for Intercultural and Interreligious Pastoral Care and Counseling (SIPCC)[1] and the International Association of Spiritual Care (IASC)[2] represent a plurality of religious, theological, and philosophical traditions. They also represent diverse disciplines and multiple professional practices within the field of pastoral and spiritual care across many social contexts. At the same time, they share a fundamental assumption that often remains implicit: that within and beyond such rich diversity, there is commonality (or universality) that makes communication and collaboration possible and, indeed, indispensable for our times.

The two main parts of this chapter consist of an exploration of common ground in both practice and theory in the field of spiritual care, broadly viewed. It thus amplifies the reference to common ground introduced in chapter 1 of this book. The first part focuses on religious communities and the search for wisdom. The question of a reappraised commonality is addressed by highlighting the universal caregiving function of these communities, as illustrated by various responses to the COVID-19 pandemic. The second part makes the case that wisdom is norm, process, and goal in spiritual care—and especially so in interfaith situations—starting with a reference to biblical tradition. The discussion is offered from a Christian perspective while inviting analogous study by colleagues who represent other religious and nonreligious traditions. The final section describes an overarching caregiving pattern that illumines the structure of wise discernment in diverse forms of spiritual care across traditions and cultures.

---

1. See SIPCC, "Mission Statement."
2. See IASC, "Mission Statement."

Common Ground

A GLOBAL CASE: THE SHARED CONTEXT OF PANDEMIC REALITIES

The global reality of the COVID-19 pandemic—with its manifold indicators of suffering—dramatically revealed the transcultural nature of our human condition. At the same time, it uncovered the human potential for compassion and solidarity. From relative *orientation* we experienced critical and, for many, traumatic *disorientation* within diverse social and cultural contexts around the world. There has subsequently also been a longing for *reorientation* toward new forms of normalcy.

At the time of this writing, more than eight hundred million cases of COVID-19 have been reported to the World Health Organization, with more than seven million deaths.[3] Such unprecedented pandemic catastrophe triggered the mobilization of international, national, and local resources to care for the population worldwide. Among private initiatives, diverse forms of pastoral and spiritual care were deployed both directly and indirectly connected with religious traditions and faith communities. Therefore, it is fitting to highlight a shared pandemic context of common concern as the overarching background for reflecting on common ground in interfaith pastoral and spiritual care.[4]

The words *pandemia* and *pandemic* come from the Greek—πάνδημος (*pándēmos*)—meaning "of, pertaining or related to all the people."[5] That being the case, in addition to applying the term to the manifestations of COVID-19, it is also appropriate to use it in connection with the reigning economic system in the world today, global market capitalism. Confronting a pandemic disease is necessarily associated with both the life-giving potential and the harmful multidimensional impact of that overarching system. At the same time, religious communities, and especially those related to the Abrahamic tradition, today can reclaim an old promise and call: "I will bless you . . . so that you will be a blessing . . . and in you all the families of the earth shall be blessed."[6] Their caregiving contributions are thus specific ways of fulfilling their pandemic vocation to become a blessing to all peoples. That is why our exploration of common ground starts with the universal caring function of religious communities.

---

3. World Health Organization, "WHO COVID-19 Dashboard."
4. See Fernandez, *Threshold Dwellers*; and Moon and Lartey, *Postcolonial Practices*.
5. Harper, "Pandemic (adj.)."
6. Gen 12:2–3.

THE UNIVERSAL CARING FUNCTION
OF RELIGIOUS COMMUNITIES

The COVID-19 pandemic impacted religious practices in various ways, including the cancellation of many worship services, pilgrimages, ceremonies, and festivals. Many places of worship were forced to close. In response, religious leaders streamed services online, allowing their followers to practice their faith in safe and socially responsible ways. Diverse groups posted online meditation sessions to help with anxiety and depression. As the coronavirus closed churches, synagogues, and mosques worldwide, religious leaders found new ways to bless millions marooned by the pandemic. Services were shared via electronic media, prayers posted by video links, and timeless texts shared on cellphones to bring spiritual support to the hundreds of thousands of believers denied a place of worship. Further, relief departments of religious organizations dispatched disinfection supplies, air-purifying respirators, face shields, gloves, coronavirus nucleic acid detection reagents, ventilators, patient monitors, syringe pumps, infusion pumps, and food to affected areas. Other faith communities offered free COVID-19 testing to the public. Adherents of many religions gathered to pray for an end to the COVID-19 pandemic, for those affected by it, as well as for wisdom for physicians and scientists to combat the disease. In sum, religious groups managed to somehow continue to experience and to practice care within and beyond their own communities. The following four claims in the manner of normative hypotheses address the questions of why and how faith communities share common ground as ecologies of care.

FOUR MAIN CLAIMS, NORMATIVE HYPOTHESES

First, *faith communities can function as mediating spaces between the cultural, socio-economic, and political realities of society at large and those of the family.* While this happens in uniquely contextualized ways, it also seems to follow a transcultural design consisting of interrelated practices of worship ("up-reach"), community life ("in-reach"), and service ministry ("out-reach"). This threefold design—worship, community, and mission—functionally defines the fundamental nature of diverse faith communities as represented in the diagram that follows. In the case of the Christian faith, this broad characterization of the church is assumed to be theologically adequate across the broad spectrum of theological traditions and denominations.

Systematic ecclesiologies can, of course, offer distinct and comprehensive theological grounding, for example, for a sacramental view articulated in Trinitarian terms.⁷

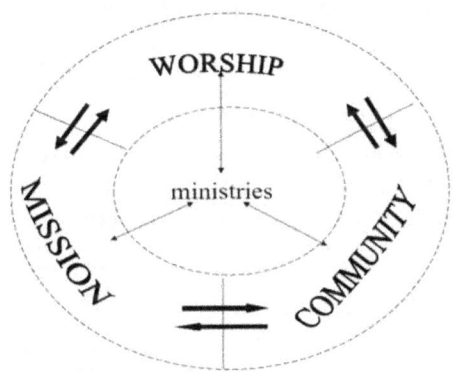

Faith communities enact the threefold love commandment.

It remains to be further explored collaboratively whether that threefold pattern is also (analogously) present in the other two "Abrahamic" faith traditions of Judaism and Islam. Ongoing interreligious collegial conversations suggest that the pattern is somehow shared by these traditions and that it might correlate with their fundamental normative theological convictions regarding love of God and love of neighbors both near and far, within and beyond the faith community. Furthermore, such understanding of faith community also connects with the view of spirit and spirituality proposed in the previous chapter. The claim is that participation in the practices of worship, community, and mission are indispensable for spiritual formation and growth in terms of meaning-making (vision-faith), communion-connectedness (virtue-love), and purpose-life project (vocation-hope).

Second, *membership and consistent participation in these religious communities are not only formative but also, at least potentially, transformative. Faith communities can thus be viewed as ecologies of nurture, support, care, and healing with unique potential in the face of sickness, trauma, and death.* Caregiving takes place both implicitly and explicitly. It happens in the ongoing participation in the life of the faith community: in worshipful celebration (prayers, confession, homilies for guidance and support, testimonies, etc.), community life (mutual prayer, visitation, support groups,

---

7. See Boff, *Trinity and Society*; and LaCugna, *God for Us*.

etc.), and service activity (material and spiritual assistance, advocacy, etc.). Caregiving can also happen more explicitly in programmatic, contextually and situationally appropriate caregiving practices, both within and beyond religious communities, as depicted in the chart that follows.

Locus	Table 3.1. Faith Community (Christian and Others) as Ecology of Care during COVID-19 and Beyond		Caregivers
	Nurturing, guiding, discerning . . . supporting, liberating, empowering . . . restoring, reconciling, healing **Caregiving focus: Primary prevention [(1) and (3)]………secondary and tertiary prevention [(2) and (4)]**		
Within the faith community	(1) • Theologically appropriate preaching and teaching adequate for all ages: about God (theodicy—a self-limiting Divine regarding power and justice yet always a compassionate companion) and evil • Scientifically and theologically adequate teaching about holistic health and stewardship of health (self-care and care for others) adequate for all ages • Optimal information about the pandemic, avoiding sickness, and preserving optimal health • Other	(2) • Theologically appropriate preaching and teaching for all ages: about God (theodicy—a self-limiting Divine regarding power and justice yet always a compassionate companion) and evil • Virtual prayer and support groups during hospitalization • Virtual visitation and counseling • Meaningful rituals and funerals • Financial and other material assistance • Other	Teachers … mentors … pastors … trained volunteers … specialized ministers
Beyond/outside the faith community	(3) • Collaboration in governmental and private ongoing efforts to prevent the spread of the virus (e.g., creating and distributing masks, disinfectants, etc.) • Advocacy regarding prevention among most vulnerable populations • Volunteering in schools, nursing homes, hospitals • Other	(4) • Emotional/spiritual support offered to neighbors (e.g., facilitating communication, transportation, etc.) and to caregivers • Financial and other material assistance available • Volunteering in schools, nursing homes, and hospitals • Funerals and other services available to the wider community • Other	

Programmatic caregiving activities.

The following caveat is in order. It is well known that faith communities can also foster toxic religion and spirituality. This is the case, for instance, in diverse forms of fundamentalism, harmful practices related to medical treatment, corrective discipline of children, and others. The challenge of spiritual toxicity is addressed in the next chapter.

Third, *faith communities can play a major role in terms of primary, secondary, and tertiary prevention*[8] *in the face of crisis and trauma.* "Primary prevention" means adequate and defensive mobilization of resources before a critical or a traumatic situation presents itself; its purpose is to hinder or neutralize the onset of a crisis or trauma resulting from such a situation. "Secondary prevention" refers to timely care made available as soon as a crisis or trauma begins to develop; in other words, it consists in prompt intervention aimed at lessening the violent impact that severe crisis or trauma always causes. "Tertiary prevention" characterizes the caregiving efforts made available to facilitate recovery and reorientation toward a "new normal."

The following graphic represents caregiving made available by faith communities correlated with the *universal pattern of orientation-disorientation-reorientation*. The dotted lines signify that movement is never smooth or consistently "forward."

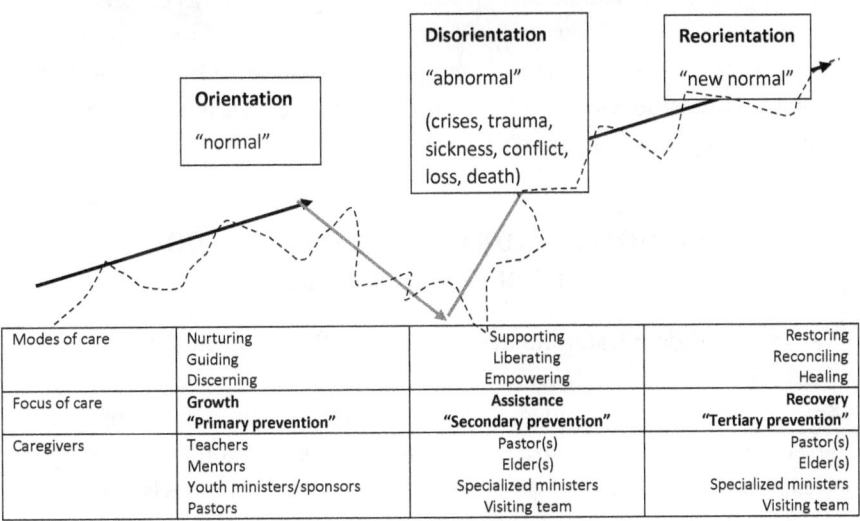

Life patterns, modes, and focus of care during COVID-19 and beyond.

8. See Caplan, *Principles of Preventive Psychiatry*.

Fourth, *comprehensive pastoral and spiritual care in response to suffering always necessitates close consideration of bio-psycho-social-spiritual factors and dynamics at play. Further, systemic strategies and approaches are always preferred. Hence, caregiving needs to be implemented together with adequate forms of communal and social-political action.* As far as care receivers' spirituality as a focus of spiritual care is concerned, both care seekers and caregivers can engage in supporting, guiding, healing, and empowering processes on different levels (family, individual, institutional, communal, and social). One of the main commonly shared goals is to foster spiritual growth in terms of meaning-making, connectedness and communion, and life orientation and purpose, as explained in the previous chapter.

Chapter 2 of this book presents a way of understanding the human spirit while also claiming that, in *spiritual* care, it is helpful to assume the universal place and function of the *human spirit* as such. Faith communities normally claim to care for people holistically—"spirit, soul, and body"—within their family, community, and the larger sociocultural context. Further, religious and theological traditions continuously address issues connected to human spirit and spirituality in more and less consistent ways. Indeed, all the world's major religious traditions have provided meaning, comfort, perspective, and sense of life direction to people for millenia. Theologian John Thatamanil explains how religions offer a comprehensive orientation, a worldview and life direction that serves as an interpretive scheme as well as a normative, therapeutic regime or pathway to healing.[9] They can thus be considered as *wisdom traditions* that inform caregiving theory and practice in manifold ways.

WISDOM AS NORM, PROCESS, AND GOAL IN SPIRITUAL CARE

Religious wisdom traditions are associated with the life of faith communities. The latter are both creators and custodians of those traditions while also being shaped, sustained, and transformed by them. Caregiving activities practiced within ("intra-faith") and in representation of ("interfaith") religious communities always connect directly with these wisdom traditions and their visions of reality and of human wholeness.

From a philosophy of science perspective, caregiving disciplines and practices such as counseling, psychotherapy, and chaplaincy are *practical*

---

9. Thatamanil, *Circling the Elephant*, 156–80.

human sciences that, like education, always must operate with norms related to the nature of reality and views of health and wholeness that orient those practices. While this characterization applies to all kinds of caregiving practice, at least implicitly, it is of course explicitly articulated in the case of religious communities and their wisdom traditions. Further, in addition to the more obvious question of caregiving goals that define the resolution or completion of a caregiving process, wisdom traditions share in common their application of a hermeneutic (interpretive) process often practiced as a way of discernment toward making wise choices. Comparative studies illustrate the distinctness as well as the commonality alluded to in the previous remarks.[10]

Recent writings explicitly represent Christian,[11] Jewish,[12] Islamic,[13] Hindu,[14] and Buddhist[15] traditions. They further help us to perceive the uniqueness and potential complementarity among those traditions. Additionally, they help us to appreciate considerable common ground in terms of normativity criteria, process, and goal. The question of normativity in spiritual care is further discussed in the appendix to this chapter.

WISDOM IN THE JUDEO-CHRISTIAN BIBLICAL TRADITION

For more than twenty years, I have worked with a model of care and counseling as a specialized form of psycho-spiritual care focused on wisdom as its ground metaphor.[16] Two main reasons undergird the proposal to reclaim wisdom as the heart of pastoral and spiritual care and counseling. First, wisdom is a significant part of the biblical tradition and of the Judeo-Christian theological heritage.[17] It represents a unique way of do-

---

10. Schipani, *Multifaith Views*.
11. See Malony and Augsburger, *Christian Counseling*.
12. See Friedman and Yehuda, *Art of Jewish Counseling*.
13. See Rassool, *Islamic Counseling*; and Ali et al., *Mantle of Mercy*.
14. See Chander and Mosher, *Hindu Approaches*.
15. See Sanford, *Kalyanamitra*.
16. Schipani, *Way of Wisdom*, 37–63.
17. See Brown, *Wisdom's Wonder*; Ceresko, *Introduction to Old Testament Wisdom*; Clements, *Wisdom in Theology*; Crenshaw, *Sipping from the Cup*; Fiddes, *Seeing the World*; Murphy, *Tree of Life*; O'Connor, *Wisdom Literature*; Penchansky, *Understanding Wisdom Literature*; Perdue, *Wisdom and Creation*; and von Rad, *Wisdom in Israel*.

ing practical theology. Second, biblically grounded wisdom language and orientation are especially suitable when redefining care and counseling as a psycho-spiritual caregiving practice. The following paragraphs explicate that rationale.

Taken as a whole, the biblical wisdom tradition presents a distinctive way of doing theology, for it deals with the fundamental questions of human existence and destiny in the light of divine action and will while focusing on everyday, mundane experience. Walter Brueggemann summarizes six aspects of scholarly consensus regarding biblical wisdom. It is, he says: (a) a theology reflecting on creation; (b) with lived experience as its data, generally not overridden by imposed interpretive categories or constructs; (c) theology in which experience is viewed as having reliability, regularity, and coherence; (d) including an unaccommodating ethical dimension; (e) a natural theology that discloses to serious discernment something of the hidden character and underpinnings of all of reality; i.e., what is given as true arises in lived experience rightly (or wisely) discerned; (f) a natural theology that reveals and discloses the God who creates, orders, and sustains reality—the generous, demanding guarantor of a viable life-order that can be trusted and counted on, but not lightly violated.[18] This tradition offers guidance for wise living through both pedagogy and counsel. It defines wise people as those who daily seek the way of wisdom and walk in that way. As Jesus is reported to have stated at the conclusion of the Sermon on the Mount, the wise are those who hear and act on the words of wisdom, thus building their house on a solid foundation.[19]

Jesus, Wisdom of God

For Christian caregivers and practical theologians, any understanding of a biblically and theologically grounded view of wisdom includes a focus on the life and ministry of Jesus. The Gospels portray him as a teacher of wisdom and a sage guided by the vision of the reign of God. Scholars suggest that he would have been seen as a Jewish prophetic sage whose message and style reflected the confluence of Hebrew sapiential, prophetic, apocalyptic, and legal forms and ideas.[20]

---

18. Brueggemann, *Theology of the Old Testament*, 680–81.
19. Matt 7:24.
20. See Witherington, *Jesus the Sage*; Borg, *Jesus*; and Borg, *Meeting Jesus Again*.

Jesus can be considered as the clue, both hermeneutically and existentially, to grasping the connection between two foundational biblical motifs: the reign of God (envisioned as normative culture and "beloved community") and wisdom in the light of God (discernment of how to live well within "beloved community" and in the larger society).[21] Jesus communicated God's alternative wisdom with an ethic and a politics of compassion reflective of divine grace. According to the four canonical gospels, his ministry thus became subversive as well as transformative and recreative because he confronted the established conventional wisdoms of his time. He challenged values, attitudes, practices, and understandings of goodness and wellness, and he transformed them.[22] Jesus's style of ministry was consistent with the wisdom tradition, and specifically with a biblically grounded wisdom in the light of God. His way of wisdom entails a counter-order—an alternative, subversive wisdom "from below."[23] Thus, he would not support today the status quo or the values of the powerful and privileged in the context of neoliberal capitalism.[24]

The relationship between Jesus as sage and Jesus as wisdom lies in the embodiment of his message. The New Testament documents, the church's teachings, and the experience of his followers point to Jesus as a living parable of God's life and wisdom. Within the larger biblical tradition, what is distinctive about Jesus is the uniquely powerful manifestation of divine wisdom in his ministry, which integrates teaching with a praxis of care, healing, empowerment, liberation, life-giving, and community building. For his followers, such caregiving and guidance thus assumes a normative, paradigmatic quality, as illustrated below.

A PARADIGMATIC STORY OF COMPANIONING IN THE FACE OF LOSS

What follows is a prototypical case taken from a sacred text of the Christian faith tradition. The post-resurrection narrative of the journey to

---

21. This is a Christian claim shared by those for whom Jesus's ministry, especially his teaching, is ethically and politically normative. Focused on care and justice, the confessional affirmations included in this section point to liberating and empowering subversion of oppressive structures and relationships on all levels.

22. Borg, *Heart of Christianity*, 80–100.

23. See Levine, *Sermon on the Mount*; and Levine, *Difficult Words of Jesus*.

24. Weiss et al., *Care, Healing, and Human Well-Being*, 144–61.

Emmaus[25] is a story whose source is about two thousand years old. It is included here because, in summary fashion, it illustrates the various points of commonality identified in this chapter, including the universal pattern of orientation-disorientation-reorientation for those who need care; the dialogical-hermeneutical process of caregiving as a way of companioning; wisdom as discernment and choice; the transforming potential of holistic engagement; and the mediating place and function of the faith community as an ecology of care.

In the story we encounter two disciples who are experiencing an overwhelming sense of loss while discussing the events leading to the tragic end of their leader by crucifixion. These two common folk are leaving Jerusalem with a sense of defeat; they are confused and plagued by doubt, fear, and anxiety. Their disillusionment is mingled with hope, however, because of news they have heard from some women of their group. They are conflicted and disoriented. The struggle for understanding motivates the two disciples to welcome the stranger, to engage him on the road, and to offer him hospitality. In sum, their open disposition and collaboration with the stranger are crucial in the ensuing work of caregiving, which in turn fosters their transformation.

As a wise caregiver, Jesus comes second in the story and does not call attention to himself. On the contrary, he becomes the disciples' neighbor by entering into their reality on their, not his, terms. He invites them to tell their story, to own their pain, and to name their crushed dreams and hopes for a better future. In due time Jesus also makes it possible for the disciples to place the social context and circumstances of their lives alongside the witness of Scripture and against the horizon of liberation in the light of God. He thus challenges conventional wisdom about the work of the promised Messiah while pointing to the grace, wisdom, and power of God, and to the paradox of the cross.

Jesus thus plays a mediating role in the interface between human experience and divine will, graciously revealed afresh. In a variety of ways, he engages the disciples holistically while inviting them to be partners in the process and respecting their freedom to make choices—for instance, when he allows them to become hosts and to share their bread [*cum panis*], thus becoming literally his *companions*. Finally, Jesus disengages at the opportune time. The disciples are reoriented and empowered to fulfill their vocation within a community that is getting ready to participate in what

25. Luke 24:13–35.

they believe is the work of God's Spirit in the world. They will testify of having faced their struggle while walking with Jesus on the road to Emmaus. Their story will thus be validated in the gathered community. In turn they will be equipped to companion others facing life's challenges and struggles both within and beyond their faith community.

This gospel story illustrates the value of sacred texts in spiritual care as special resources stemming from religious traditions. Such texts, available in all traditions, can not only inform and inspire but also supply direction to both the theory and the practice of spiritual caregiving.

UNDERSTANDING AND PRACTICING WISDOM

Biblically grounded and theologically viewed notions of wisdom blend moral and spiritual dimensions, by presenting wisdom and becoming wise as living in accordance with the knowledge and the love of God. Further, divine wisdom is acknowledged as the ultimate ground and goal of our human endeavors to sponsor wholeness and fullness of life.[26] In sum, wisdom is the heart of spiritual care, which fundamentally calls for awakening, nurturing, and developing people's *moral and spiritual intelligence*.[27] Caregiving is a unique setting that offers the possibility of becoming wiser, an extraordinary place and situation where formation and transformation are expected to happen ultimately as a divine gift.

Christian practical theologians have recently offered views on, and applications of, existential and practical wisdom consistent with the notions

---

26. Pastoral and spiritual caregivers can work with a view of reality that is not only two-dimensional (i.e., only as a matter of people in their environment/social context/world) as explained in the first chapter of this book. They can acknowledge the dimensions of abundant life and grace and the threat of "not being" and evil. Further, they can realize that knowing deeply in ways that foster guidance, support, liberation, and healing requires attending to the four dimensions. It is in that light that spiritual care aims at awakening, nurturing, and developing people's moral and spiritual intelligence (as described in the next footnote), that is, living well in the face of life's challenges and struggles.

27. The concept of "moral and spiritual intelligence" is connected to the main understanding of *wisdom* as a holistic way of knowing that includes discernment, making good choices, and living well in community. From a psychological point of view, there is abundant support for such understanding. See Sternberg and Glück, *Cambridge Handbook on Wisdom*; and Sternberg and Glück, *Psychology of Wisdom*. It is also the case with main tenets of positive psychology. See Keyes and Haidt, *Flourishing*; and Peterson and Seligman, *Character Strengths and Virtues*.

articulated in the previous paragraphs.[28] For their part, researchers on the philosophy and psychology of wisdom coincide on highlighting the essential spiritual-moral dimension of wisdom.[29]

DISCERNMENT AS PRACTICAL WISDOM

Discernment defines wisdom as an indispensable practice and discipline. Becoming wiser always involves the disposition and the capacity to discern not only the better means to reach our life goals, but especially which goals are truly worth valuing and seeking. More specifically, discerning the way of wisdom is essential when one is confronted with existential challenges (for example, needing to make or change key vocational decisions) and struggles (for instance, facing the tragic death of a loved one). Discernment, including deliberation and judgment, is thus key to both process and content in spiritual caregiving, and it must be seen and guided as inseparable from the outcome(s) being sought (for example, making and implementing an important vocational decision, grieving in a wholesome way, and healing). Put in the simplest terms, we behave wisely whenever we are able to discern what is the right thing to do, and act in such a way as to bring this about. In spiritual care, goals (caregiving objectives, expected outcomes, or *what for*) ought to be considered together with discernment as key to the questions of process (caregiving methods, strategy, or *how*) and content (agreed-on caregiving focus, or *what*). The main role of the caregiver is to guide the process, for guidance and wisdom go hand in hand, and discernment is always key.[30]

---

28. See Bass and Dykstra, *For Life Abundant*; and Bass, et al., *Christian Practical Wisdom*. It should be noted that our understanding of wisdom (*sophia*), which includes apprehension and appreciation as well as critical reflection and an orientation to practice based on life experience, incorporates the Aristotelian notion of practical reason and knowledge with moral import and ends *(phronesis)*.

29. See Hall, *Wisdom*; Boelhower, *Choose Wisely*; Sternberg and Glück, *Cambridge Handbook on Wisdom*; and Sternberg and Glück, *Psychology of Wisdom*. See also Chittister, *Welcome to the Wisdom of the World*.

30. There is indeed an interesting connection between *wisdom* and *guidance* in light of etymological considerations. The word *guide* comes from an ancient Romanic word, *widare*, which means *to know*. The words *wise, wisdom, wit,* and *guide* all share the same origin.

SPIRITUAL CARE AND CROSS-CULTURAL PATTERNS OF WISE DISCERNMENT

Most kinds of caregiving situations—particularly counseling, psychotherapy, and chaplaincy—involve patterned partnerships. They are encounters in which time and effort are invested in companioning as manifold expressions of therapeutic love and caregiving power. This reference to power is clarified below.

Caregiving relationships are always asymmetrical and differentiated by roles and context as far as personal power is concerned. In all kinds of situations, competent caregivers can practice a special form of power, whether power *with* (collaboration, co-creation of meaning), power *for* (support, guidance, empowering), power *over* (e.g., prevention of abuse, self-harm), or power *against* (e.g., confronting falsehood, unjustice). These power dynamics can also be connected with a process-relational understanding of *agential* and *receptive* power. *Agential* power—the capacity to influence and initiate—normally employs directive and guiding communication styles along with informing and asking skills; *receptive* power—the capacity to be influenced and changed by what comes to us—typically uses following styles along with listening skills.[31] The power and authority of caregivers is thus connected to a unique form of love of neighbor that helps define the therapeutic alliance. It is with such understanding of spiritual caregiving that we can now proceed to describe a fundamental process.

A FIVE-STEP PARADIGM

On the one hand, it is possible to trace developments in the specific ways that caregiving relationships have been structured and performed through the centuries and across cultures. On the other hand, it is also possible to identify persistent continuity in basic pattern(s) of caregiving practice. The work of practical theologian Maria Harris regarding teaching and religious imagination unveils a remarkable analogy to the fundamental form (*Gestalt*) of spiritual caregiving relationships depicted in the graphic below.[32] Diverse kinds of spiritual care in counseling and psychotherapy, chaplaincy, narrative medicine, and others can be reimagined as special manifestations of wise discernment practiced analogously to this patterned process.

---

31. Doehring, *Practice of Pastoral Care*, 44–46.
32. Harris, *Teaching and Religious Imagination*, 23–40.

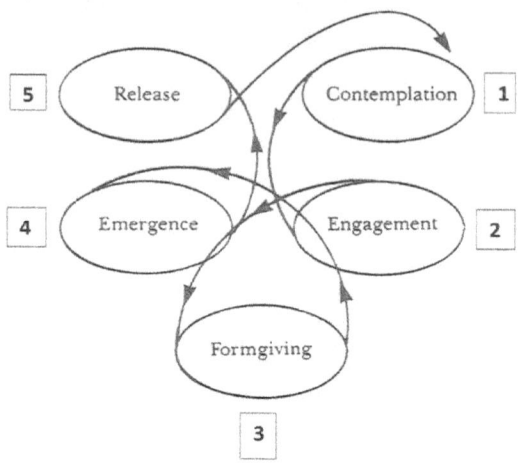

A five-step paradigm in spiritual care.

The first moment in competent pastoral and spiritual care is *contemplation*, as manifest in religious imagination. It is an attitude of respect, appreciation, receptivity, and curious reverence; it is being free from preoccupation and preconception. Such welcoming, gracious openness is often reciprocated by care receivers. Caregivers also contemplate the actual caregiving event and themselves and, perhaps, also the Source of grace, wisdom, and power with which/Whom they work. Thus understood, contemplation remains as an indispensable disposition that defines the quality of presence (or, "being present") and active listening throughout the caregiving process.

Engagement is the second step or moment in the pattern. It defines the kind of interaction and interchange involved in getting acquainted, clarifying expectations with psycho-spiritual assessment, and establishing goals and boundaries in the caregiving relationship. Co-creating trust-infused therapeutic alliances, broadly and narrowly speaking, is essential. The quality of rapport that is generated facilitates the therapeutic conversation focused on the care receivers' agenda, and their needs and potential to move toward reorientation.[33] *Formgiving* in turn names the dialectical, co-creating activity of searching for meaning and clarity, and for the path

---

33. From the perspective of those needing care, under all kinds of circumstances the fundamental, universal pattern always consists in a process moving from (relative) orientation to disorientation to seeking reorientation. Such fundamental pattern is typically illustrated in sacred scriptures such as the Psalms, and the lament psalms in particular. See Brueggemann, *Spirituality of the Psalms*.

to some form of resolution in the face of the specific life's challenges and struggles that made caregiving necessary. It does so by activating internal and external resources for such purpose. This moment of discernment is normally oriented to making wise decisions for the way forward in light of shared criteria of human wholeness and flourishing life in community.

As a result of the dialogical and hermeneutical work of formgiving, *emergence* happens as care receivers realize that they can find themselves in a new and better place in their life journey. This moment usually includes appropriate verification that, indeed, some form of resolution has taken place, or is taking place. (Necessary emergence thus viewed cannot be guaranteed, and should not be rushed by caregivers. Neither should the caregiving process be prolonged beyond the sought-for resolution or reorientation.) Opportune *release* is, therefore, a necessary final moment in the caregiving relationship. In all kinds of fruitful caregiving processes, release is the step that marks the culmination of such partnership.

Many caregivers have explicitly adopted and adapted this pattern in spiritual caregiving practice. It should be noted that the pattern is analogous to the fundamental structure and dynamics of artwork of different kinds, such as sculpting, painting, music composition, writing, and many others. It nicely fits the description and explanation of the creative process.[34] Also, given this author's Argentine identity and cultural background, it can be added that *tango* music and dance offer a similarly helpful analogy. On the one hand, tango dancing uniquely represents key caregiving principles such as asymmetry, rapport, optimal distance (or nearness, intimacy), improvisation and co-creation of form and content, and timing. On the other hand, its aesthetic structure is also analogous to the five-step pattern described in this section.[35]

Readers are invited to consider such a pattern of creative process as a recognizable structure in their clinical work and in the reflection on caregiving practice. In other words, the question is also whether diverse forms of spiritual care can be thus reimagined as unique manifestations of structured wise discernment.

---

34. See Koestler, *Act of Creation*.

35. Interesting illustrations of the analogy can be observed in the cases of two couples dancing to the melody of the same musical piece—"Por Una Cabeza," a classic Argentine tango—in two well-known films. While keeping in mind the pattern described in this section, readers can compare Madonna and Antonio Banderas in *Evita* with Al Pacino and Gabrielle Anwar in *The Scent of a Woman*. See Parker, *Evita*; and Brest, *Scent of a Woman*.

RECAPITULATION

This chapter presents detailed explications of three sets of claims of commonality in spiritual care practice and theory that were briefly mentioned in chapter 1. The first has to do with the place and role of religious communities as bearers of wisdom traditions, viewed in light of the COVID-19 pandemic and beyond. The second concerns the question of wisdom as norm, process, and goal. The third refers to an overarching caregiving pattern of discernment understood as practical wisdom.

First, the universal caring function of religious communities can be appreciated in terms of both a fundamental structure that has "up-reach," "in-reach," and "out-reach" dimensions, and as intentional commitment to caregiving practices. These communities are shaped by wisdom traditions that serve as the foundation for their spiritual formation and for their manifold practices of care in the face of suffering. Further, religious communities can offer support as well as accountability to all caregivers associated with them.

Second, diverse spiritual and religious traditions have explicitly addressed the spiritual dimension and existential quests throughout millennia, as documented in sacred texts and other artifacts. They can be called *wisdom traditions* because they offer ways to growth in wisdom (or *spiritual and moral intelligence*) and human wholeness. Philosophical and theological traditions started much later to also explicitly articulate questions related to the spiritual dimension. And, it must be added, the systematic study of and engagement with the spiritual dimension in the social and behavioral sciences, and in clinical psychology in particular, is relatively recent.

Third, throughout the ages and across cultures, diverse forms of caregiving practice have been available in order to focus on, engage, guide, support, reorient, and/or heal the human spirit thus understood. Fundamentally, *as a compassionate response to human suffering,*[36] *spiritual care is a special way of companioning; and all forms of spiritual care have always consisted in connecting wisdom traditions with care receivers' spiritual resources, longings, and struggles in sociocultural and contextually pertinent ways.* Such can be, therefore, a broad response to the question, "What is spiritual care?" Multiple forms of dialogical-narrative and hermeneutical process are normally involved in such companioning where discernment unfolds as practical wisdom.

---

36. In this context and broadly speaking, *suffering* can be understood as "dis-ease," that is, "disturbance of ease" in situations ranging from mild disorientation to severe trauma.

APPENDIX: NORMATIVITY AT THE CENTER IN SPIRITUAL CARE

Normativity was addressed in chapter 1 of this book with an interdisciplinary approach to psycho-spiritual assessment. It was noted that by using psychological and theological norms it is possible to determine whether certain clinical approaches are "psychologically functional" and "theologically adequate"; the same can be done regarding care receivers' spiritual experiences and activities. Another important point was the presentation of two different models—"foundational" and "correlational or dialogical"[37]—for connecting psychological and theological views and resources in spiritual care. It was clarified that the normative framework can also be philosophical-ethical and non-theistic. In chapter 2, normativity was considered in connection with the relationship between mental and spiritual health.

Recognition of normativity is indispensable because criteria are needed for assessment, for the ongoing appraisal of progress in the caregiving process, and for evaluating the caregiving practice as such. Those criteria relate to a constellation of values[38] within a clinical (broadly speaking) framework and a visional-ethical schema. The resulting guiding principles—dependable guides to practice—are obviously essential in all forms of caregiving activity. Normativity illumines the answers we give to many questions. What is going on psycho-spiritually? How are improvement, healing, or satisfactory resolution determined? What is a good or desirable outcome? How effectively and appropriately are the caregiving approaches employed? How well are interdisciplinary frameworks, views, and resources, including those of our philosophical or religious traditions, applied? And so on.

37. Doehring, "Challenges of Being Bilingual."

38. Counselors, psychotherapists, medical doctors, nurses, and other caregivers normally acknowledge the central place of ethics and moral reasoning in their work. Ethics are foundational to caregiving and guide decisions regarding best practices and working in the best interests of care receivers. Regardless of specific work setting, caregivers face ethical dilemmas in their daily work. They must be able to reason ethically through challenging situations and determine the most appropriate course of action that ultimately is in the best interests of those cared for. This requires awareness of professional and personal issues influencing their decisions. Value-laden decisions and actions are informed by values stemming from deeply held, intimate beliefs that are moral, religious, or cultural in nature. Undoubtedly, values not only enter the caregiving relationship, but also greatly impact many different facets of the relationship. It should be clear that, together with "professional ethics" strictly speaking, we have in mind those norms regarding what is desirable and life-giving change, or "moving forward," in any caregiving situation.

Just as in the case of other practical human disciplines such as education, consideration and application of norms is essential. There is no such thing as metaphysical, ethical, and epistemological neutrality on the part of pastoral and spiritual caregivers. They must be critically aware of the (implicit and/or explicit) normativity that informs their caregiving practice and theory—that is, the norms and standards supplied by both behavioral-social science and philosophical or theological traditions. A complicating factor is that the behavioral and social sciences are themselves connected to certain wisdom traditions with their metaphysical claims and ethical visions.[39]

Reflection on normativity in spiritual care includes yet an additional epistemological question. It has to do with explicitly integrating particular visional-ethical schema from diverse wisdom traditions into a single theory. This is the case of philosophical psychologies, as in Buddhist contributions.[40] And it is also the case of religious-theological psychologies, some of which function as particular psycho-theologies for spiritual care, such as Christian,[41] Islamic,[42] and Hindu.[43]

It is with a shared understanding of normativity, one which embraces both commonality and particularity connected with diverse wisdom

---

39. Browning systematically unveils the implicit, or "hidden," metaphysical assumptions and ethical visions of major modern psychologies. Concerning the relationship between theology and psychology, he states: "Insofar as the modern psychologies achieve the status of scientific knowledge (either clinical or experimental), logically they should not conflict with the claims of theology . . . psychology can only conflict with theology when psychology in some way ceases to be properly scientific (however this is defined) and drifts over into normative language of either ethical or metaphysical kind." Browning, *Religious Thought*, 6–15.

40. See Kornfield, *Wise Heart*; Levine, *Positive Psychology of Buddhism and Yoga*; and Sanford, *Kalyanamitra*.

41. See McMinn, *Psychology, Theology, and Spirituality*; Moriarti, *Integrating Faith and Psychology*; Roberts and Talbot, *Limning the Psyche*; Sandage and Brown, *Relational Integration of Psychology*; and Entwistle, *Integrative Approaches to Psychology*. For several decades now, Christian psychologists, counselors, and pastoral and spiritual caregivers, as well as pastoral/practical theologians, have articulated ways to understand and clinically apply connections and correlations involving psychology and theology, and possible "integrations" of those disciplines in theory and practice. As expected, those proposals always include explicit reference to a Christian worldview and philosophy of life as well as specific ethical considerations. A similar appraisal is of course applicable to contributions stemming from other religious/theological traditions such as Hinduism and Islam.

42. See Al-Karam, *Islamically Integrated Psychotherapy*; Isgandarova, *Islamic Spiritual and Religious Care*; and Rothman, *Developing a Model of Islamic Psychology*.

43. See Chander and Mosher, *Hindu Approaches*.

traditions, that spiritual caregivers engage in various forms of spiritual care in multiple settings. This understanding is also indispensable to caring well in interfaith situations and to collaborating across traditions and disciplines with collegial commitment.

The discussion of normativity serves as a necessary preface for approaching the question of spiritual harm and struggle briefly alluded to in chapter 2. To that topic, undoubtedly a major concern of spiritual caregivers across traditions and professions, we now turn our attention.

4

Spiritual Distress

Toxicity, Struggle, and Injury

UNDERSTANDINGS OF PSYCHO-SPIRITUAL WHOLENESS can be found in diverse sources, including the contributions of Positive Psychology.[1] Counselors and psychotherapists also offer valuable input regarding the differences between healthy and harmful/toxic spirituality. Criteria for the former include: an embodied sense of identity, worth, and value together with the experience and cultivation of loving relationships; a trustworthy and friendly sense of connection and belonging; support for positive character traits, especially compassion and empathy, secure attachment, and a moral compass; and lived and transcendent meaning, especially in the face of adversity.[2]

This chapter focuses on some of the serious threats to psycho-spiritual wholeness, beginning with a case study from an Islamic spiritual care perspective. It is followed by a discussion and assessment of religious fundamentalism as inherently toxic spirituality. Such evaluation is then applied to spiritual-political toxicity as present in Christian nationalism and white supremacy ideology and politics. There follows a section on understanding spiritual struggles and moral injury as a special focus for spiritual care, leading to visualizing transformation as the overarching goal for recovery and healing.

A MUSLIM CAREGIVER ADDRESSES TOXIC SPIRITUALITY

Nazila Isgandarova is a Muslim psychotherapist and a leading voice in the growing chorus of Islamic caregivers, theorists, and practical theologians.

---

1. See Csikszentmihalyi and Csikszentmihalyi, *Life Worth Living*; and Lopez and Snyder, *Oxford Handbook of Positive Psychology*.
2. Benner, *Soulful Spirituality*, 4–7, 21–26, 72–77; and Jones, *Spirit in Session*, 139–44.

A focus of concern for her has been unhealthy spirituality that characterizes one's experience of domestic violence as a situation of "divine testing and suffering" and "spiritual disease and distress."[3] What follows is the story of a woman whose unhealthy practices included self-sacrifice, resistance to active treatment for her illness, and enduring suffering due to domestic violence. Says Isgandarova, "situations like this lead me to explore how serious misunderstanding of the theology of evil and suffering, divine predetermination, God's omnipotence and justice contributes to unhealthy spiritual practices among Muslims."[4]

Asma had a passive attitude toward the domestic violence she had experienced. Her hope was to achieve higher spiritual rewards for her endurance and acceptance of her husband's abusive behavior, according to her interpretation of the Qur'an. She married her husband when she was seventeen in order to escape family duties, but her marriage was neither satisfactory nor happy. In addition to physically abusing her, her husband betrayed her emotionally with someone very close to her. Asma did not divorce her husband because of their two children and because she simply did not want to return to her parents' home. She suffered from depression related to the abuse and infidelity.

All these life experiences caused deep wounds in Asma's spirit, soul, and body. She didn't want to continue treatment in a hospital and didn't want to take a prescribed antidepressant medication. She believed that her *chilla* (suffering) was retribution for past sins and for not being consistent in following the prescribed five daily ritual prayers of Islam. She followed the advice of a female mentor in a weekly spirituality group who told her

---

3. Isgandarova, *Muslim Women*, 72–94, 122–44. The book is a practical theological inquiry about the lived experience of the Islamic tradition and its application in psychotherapy with Muslim women subject to domestic violence. Isgandarova's psychotherapeutic approach consists of a five-step process (DEEDS) as follows: *describe* the problem (assessment of spiritual distress); *examine* factors involved from the Islamic tradition; *explore* insights from the social sciences; *develop* a spiritual care plan that addresses the problem and empowers Muslim women to take appropriate action; and *suggest* Islamic psychotherapeutic interventions that focus on the "spiritual diagnosis"—drawing upon Shari'ah, Islamic theology, Sufism, and contemporary psychotherapy theories as well as resources from within the community (12). As a Muslim psychotherapist, Isgandarova correlates an Islamic theological normative framework with appropriate clinical approaches from existential, transpersonal, and cognitive behavior therapy, among others.

4. Undated personal communication. I am grateful for conversation and collaboration with Dr. Isgandarova. A version of the case of "Asma" is found in Isgandarova, *Muslim Women*, 72–86, 88–91. Unless otherwise documented, the rest of this section has material from our collegial interactions, including a sample verbatim, in addition to the references from her published text.

that if she grew in her faith, her suffering would diminish. She had been told to show *sabr* (endurance, patience) in her pain, suffering, and difficult life and to know that her *sabr* to her husband's abusive behavior was one-half of her religion (the other half being gratitude to God, as mentioned in the *hadith* or sayings and practices of the Prophet Muhammad*)*. She often recited verses about the virtue of steadfastness: "God loves the patient," and "surely God is with the patient."[5] She was also comforted by a prophetic *hadith,* "Patience toward suffering is an essential character of the believers, for they know that the real cause and goal of suffering is God: among humankind, those who are stricken with the most terrible of misfortunes are the Prophets, and then follow others according to their degree of faith."

Isgandarova recalls the challenge of therapeutic transference and resistance: "As a therapeutic style, I tried to provide an empathic stance as much as possible. There were times when I found it difficult to maintain an empathic stance when the client talked about her tolerance to abuse. However, I realized that any comment on this might shift the process to fit my own agenda and associations. For me, at this stage the patient's point of view was the most important." A segment of the caregiving dialogue follows.

> Therapist: Is there any other reason that you don't want to take an antidepressant?
>
> Asma: [Silence.] I don't know . . . I don't think I feel comfortable taking it.
>
> Therapist: Can you help me understand what you mean when you say that you are not comfortable?
>
> Asma: I don't feel safe. I'm afraid it may have an adverse effect or that I will be addicted to it. I think doctors tend to overprescribe medication for me.
>
> Therapist: So, it means you don't want drug therapy. What do you think can help you?
>
> Asma: I'm comfortable with someone listening to me without asking too many questions. I think they might find me strange when I tell them that I believe what happened to me is because of my past sins. Often they insist on asking me how I accept my husband's emotional affair and physical abuse. [Her eyes become watery and her voice breaks as she tells the details of her husband's

---

5. Qur'an 3.145 and 2.153.

affair.] Of course, I don't mean that his betrayal didn't hurt me. I was let down and feel sad and lonely when I remember. I didn't expect him to betray me—he is Muslim. When I told my doctor about his illicit relationship, she thought that it would be better if I left him in order to stop the cycle of abuse. But then my *abla* [in Turkish, "big sister," or in religious circles, a female mentor or teacher] said that it might be my *chilla* and test of Allah, which is why it is better if I accept what happened to me. She advised me to pray and ask God for forgiveness for myself and for him. She also prayed with me and read from this book [she points to a book[6]] that any trial that falls upon the believer wipes away his or her sins.

Therapist: How did you feel when your *abla* suggested that you should be patient?

Asma: [She takes a deep breath.] Do I have any other choice? I know that, although everything comes from Allah, at least Allah is with me no matter what happens. So, I don't question Allah because of my husband's behavior; he is a means in the divine hand. Allah has a plan for me.

Therapist: Do you mean that your husband's emotional affair and abuse sometimes is a divine trial? How do you feel when you say that?

Asma: I don't feel so good. Who wants to endure such a trial? But it is my *qadar* [divine destiny] to be betrayed, and what is expected from me is to be patient and wait. I will be rewarded for my patience. I don't have any other choice . . . I cannot control my *qadar*.

Therapist: Asma, I am trying to understand you. As a woman, of course I also would not want to endure such a trial. You mentioned that you believe that your husband is a "means" or a part of the "divine hand." When you describe your husband in this way, does it mean that you don't have expectations from your husband for, for example, fairness or good treatment?

Asma: Of course, I want him to treat me fairly. I wish he were more intimate with me. But I know that if he does not treat me well, then I am sure that what suffering comes from Allah [she does not say, suffering that comes from her husband] I will be rewarded for it.

---

6. Gülen, *Emerald Hills*.

Allah will answer my prayers in the end. [Her eyes look sad, and her body is tense.]

Therapist: I really admire your resilience and forgiveness—these are positive traits that may act as a buffer during your hard times. What helps enhance your resilience? What helps you refuse to accept negative messages from your environment and your husband?[7]

Asma's passive attitude toward her husband's behavior—and toward her own resulting depression—stemmed from both her belief in a coming reward from God and her fear of being a disobedient wife, which she strongly believed would lower her spiritual status. She reported that her continuing trust in God had manifold results: steadfastness in performing her prayers, endurance in the face of difficulties—regardless of the severity of the pain—and ability to fulfill her spousal duties toward her husband in order to please him. She found the endurance shown by great prophets and saints in their afflictions as a model for her own behavior. She especially liked to narrate the story of the prophet Job who, despite his contagious disease and the loss of family members and wealth, did not abandon his hope in God's compassion and mercy.[8]

A number of spiritual counseling issues arose regarding Asma's understanding of her depression and the domestic abuse that she experienced, due to the unhealthy spirituality at work. Indicators of this toxicity included a belief in the virtue of necessary suffering by interpreting it as a test from God; tolerance toward domestic violence; and refusal of professional treatment for her depression, due to the perception that mental as well as physical health problems were a test from God, as well as a lack of trust in current clinical treatment options for depression.[9]

---

7. Psychotherapy with a Muslim caregiver helped Asma strengthen her faith and improve her character as a Muslim; and she learned how a strong faith made her resilient. Asma was struggling to know whether her experience of domestic violence was part of her faith, and whether her test was due to God's anger towards her, or due to God's love. Isgandarova, *Muslim Women*, 73.

8. Qur'an 21:83; 13:86, 38:44.

9. Isgandarova explains that the Qur'an does not discourage believers from being passive when they are challenged by pain and suffering as a "divine" test. Rather, the Qur'an teaches that *sabr* (endurance, patience) helps in a situation when the weak and powerless do not have enough resources to change their situation. She also asserts that it is not, however, helpful to assume a victim's helplessness when the afflicted may have access to internal and external resources to challenge evil that causes their suffering.

Isgandarova asserts that viewing suffering as a virtue, and as a means to achieve higher spiritual ranks, fosters unhealthy spiritual practices and undergirds the subordinate role of Muslim women. She adds that submissiveness of Muslim women to suffering can be traced back to the influence of dominant Islamic theologies of suffering. She also critically surveys diverse Islamic theological schools, and theodicies in particular, together with Islamic feminist perspectives to further illumine Asma's predicament and the way forward toward healing.[10]

FUNDAMENTALISM AS TOXIC SPIRITUALITY

Abrahamic religions lend themselves to fundamentalism[11] because of the emphasis on orthodoxy and orthopraxy—right belief and right action.[12] In other words, they center on the idea of scriptural norms for doctrine, ethics, politics, and society.[13] These traditions work from a place of "scriptural revelations" that, for them, have political, moral, and social implications and "form the corpus of demands."[14] Other religious traditions do not hold scriptural or doctrinal allegiance at the center of their organization or ideology and tend to instead uphold "national or cultural purity" in religious-political movements. For example, certain Buddhist, Sikh, and Hindu groups can aggressively and sometimes violently emphasize nationalistic political ideologies rather than doctrinal religious-political ideologies.[15]

In all cases it is important to realize that fundamentalist movements have come about through different historical experiences and reactions. At the same time, the overarching claim has been made that what these

---

10. Isgandarova highlights liberating Islamic interpretations of suffering, especially in relation to social justice and human rights. Those views emphasize the importance of freedom of choice and invite people to question the source of their suffering, whether it is from God or from humans, while encouraging resistance to unnecessary suffering and affirming responsibility for human destiny. Isgandarova, *Muslim Women*, 73–83.

11. The term "fundamentalism" was coined in the United States in the early twentieth century and, since its beginnings a century ago, it has come to be woven into the religious vocabulary of various faith traditions. Lechner, "Fundamentalism," 197. See also Antoun, *Understanding Fundamentalism*.

12. Partridge, *Fundamentalisms*, 7.

13. Partridge, *Fundamentalisms*, 16.

14. Partridge, *Fundamentalisms*, 11; see also Hood, *Psychology of Religious Fundamentalism*.

15. Partridge, *Fundamentalisms*, 10–11.

movements have in common is that they have turned the *mythos* of their religion into *logos*, either by insisting that their dogmas are scientifically true or by transforming their complex mythology into a streamlined ideology. Karen Armstrong concludes that fundamentalist movements are rooted in a fear of imminent annihilation.[16] From a spiritual health science viewpoint, we focus on the structure and dynamics characteristic of all forms of fundamentalism, as follows: a markedly strict literalism as applied to specific scriptures, dogmas, or ideologies; a strong effort to maintain in-group and out-group distinctions; and, in many but not all cases, an assertive and sometimes violent "missional" impulse and orientation. We can demonstrate that most forms of fundamentalism foster toxic spirituality because they are closed systems that harm the human spirit in recognizable ways; further, that fundamentalisms tend to nurture and support diverse forms of violence,[17] and violent extremism in particular.[18]

"RELIGIOUS TRAUMA SYNDROME"

People who have experienced transformation as a conversion toward healing report having suffered what is called Religious Trauma Syndrome (RTS). This constellation of symptoms refers to the experience shared among many who have escaped cults, fundamentalist religious groups, abusive religious settings, or other painful experiences with religion. While not an official psychiatric diagnosis, RTS is a function of both the chronic abuses of harmful religion and the impact of severing the connection with one's faith and faith community. The trauma consists in a huge systemic shock on personal, family, and communal levels. RTS is the condition experienced by people who struggle with leaving an authoritarian, dogmatic religion and must cope with the damage of indoctrination and harmful practices. They typically go through the shattering of a personally meaningful faith and/or breaking away from a controlling community and lifestyle. Indicators of RTS may include, among others: confusing thoughts and reduced ability to think critically; negative beliefs about self, others, and the world; trouble making decisions; feelings of depression, anxiety, grief, anger, and lethargy;

---

16. Armstrong, *Battle for God*, 366–68.

17. Violence is here defined as the human exercise of physical, emotional, spiritual, social, or technological power that results in injury or harm to others or oneself. All forms of human violence can thus be characterized as abuse of power.

18. Schipani, "Fundamentalism as Toxic Spirituality."

a sense of feeling lost, directionless, and alone; a lack of pleasure or interest in things one used to enjoy; a loss of a community (family, friends, romantic relationships); and a feeling of isolation or a sense of not belonging. Recovery always involves a laborious reorientation and healing process.[19]

The tragic story of the Peoples Temple illustrates the potentially lethal outcome of religious violent extremism. It also demonstrates the significant role of authoritarian leadership complicated and enhanced by a leader's mental disorder.

THE CASE OF THE PEOPLES TEMPLE[20]

On November 18, 1978, 919 people—including 276 children—died in Jonestown, Guyana. Except for U.S. Representative Leo Ryan and the party who accompanied him to South America on a fact-finding mission and who were killed by armed Temple members, the rest died in what had been planned and described by Reverend Jim Jones as "revolutionary suicide." The event marked the collapse of an ill-fated project fashioned under the banner of apostolic socialism. It was the largest and most notorious murder-suicide in American (that is, in Latin America and United States) history.

Jim Jones and his team had imagined that the closed community—Peoples Temple—would become a utopic sanctuary and socialist paradise. However, Jones's leadership became more and more authoritarian as his mental health continued to deteriorate. The testimony of surviving followers includes a record of diverse forms of physical, emotional, and spiritual violence. Eventually, violence perpetrated against suspected outsiders and those seeking to escape also engulfed the whole community in a final act of self-destruction.

19. Pasquale, *Sacred Wounds*.

20. The faith community known as the Peoples Temple was founded by the Rev. Jim Jones in Indianapolis in 1956 and was associated originally with the Disciples of Christ denomination. It was conceived as an integrated church with a strong communitarian vision and a focus on caring and advocating for oppressed people. Jones developed the ideology of "apostolic socialism" by combining tenets of the Christian prophetic tradition with socialist ideals. He also blended social concerns with faith healing and "charismatic" worship services drawn from the Black church experience. In the 1960s he moved the congregation to California, where he established several locations gathering thousands of followers. In 1974, after a number of significant achievements and public recognitions as well as political conflicts, scandals, and adverse publicity, Jones and his team moved the community to Guyana, in South America. The vision was to create the "Peoples Temple Agricultural Project" in the area informally renamed "Jonestown."

There have been numerous studies focusing on this tragedy. All of them highlight the lethal effect of consistently fostered toxic spirituality among people searching for significance, belonging, and a sense of purpose. Ultimately, their fate was sealed under Jones's megalomaniac, paranoid, and authoritarian leadership.[21]

SPIRITUAL TOXICITY AND FUNDAMENTALISM

Unhealthy spiritualities express themselves in terms of beliefs, attitudes, relationships, and practices with different degrees of toxicity. Further, they also include a measure of violence and, often, a form of power or abuse that harms or injures the self and/or others. Such violence can be emotional, spiritual/moral, and, sometimes, physical including sexual violence. Further, these dimensions and degrees of violence can be appraised on a spectrum in which harm goes from relatively minor to lethal.

Spiritual toxicity undermines emotional/mental health, and it does so without exceptions. Further, family systems and faith communities severely affected by toxic spirituality usually show habitual patterns of behavior that can be characterized as "hamster wheel syndrome," describable as "running in circles."[22] It must be also acknowledged that both religious and nonreligious spiritualities[23] can become toxic.

APPLYING INTERDISCIPLINARY LENSES

By employing interdisciplinary lenses and psychological and theological norms introduced in chapter 1, we find that fundamentalist spiritualities can never be "healthy" even when they are psycho-sociologically functional. The following chart helps us to identify four possibilities. It may also help to visualize the process from fundamentalist oppression to healing. The graphic intentionally includes references to political and military forms

---

21. See Guinn, *Road to Jonestown*.
22. See Engelmann, *Running in Circles*.
23. For example, my ongoing work with training prison and hospital chaplains in Cuba regularly includes the appraisal of an ideologically appropriated, secularized spirituality consistently promoted by the government in the public education system of that country. Christian chaplains must therefore develop intercultural and interfaith competence in order to adequately engage care receivers spiritually on their own terms. See Bidwell and Schipani, "Interreligious Care in Totalitarian Contexts."

of toxic spirituality, which are also viewed as closed systems and which will be discussed in the next sections of this chapter.

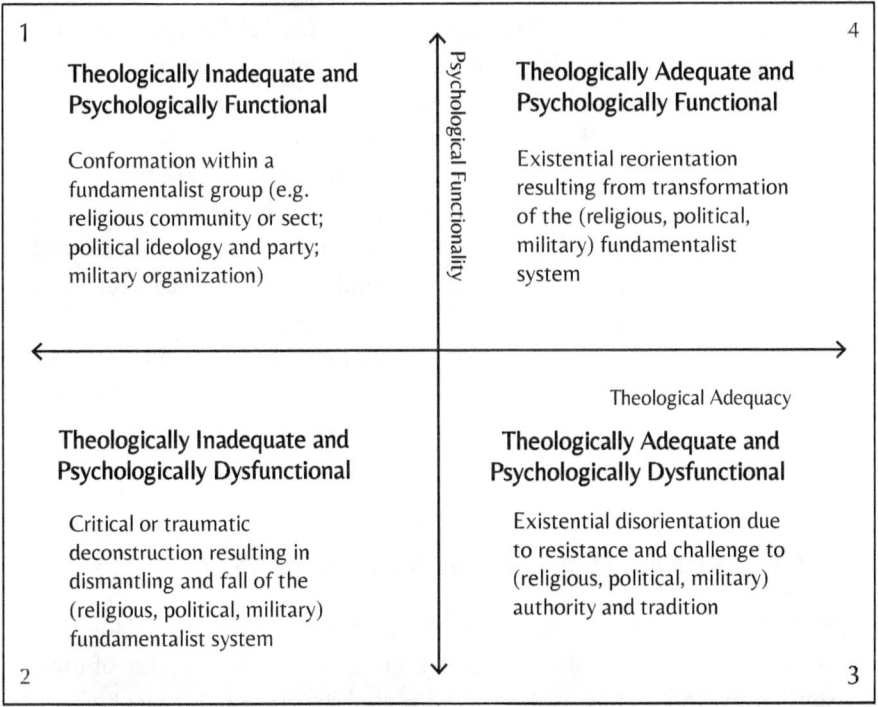

Assessing toxic spirituality with interdisciplinary lenses.

Quadrant 1 represents the case of psychological functionality and theological inadequacy, the latter so judged by those leaving the community, tradition, or militant group. The former involves primarily the multiple psychological benefits of belonging to a certain group, such as an extreme Islamist organization. The decision to leave the system, however, always involves a major collapse because of psychological dysfunctionality and/or theological inadequacy, as indicated in quadrant 2. Moving away physically and ideologically typically results in measures of dysfunctionality—existential disorientation—related to the loss of former integration; in addition, there might follow rejection, punishment, or persecution by those remaining in the system, as suggested in quadrant 3. Finally, existential reorientation can happen as people move toward, and find a place within, a healthier communal-social environment, as described in quadrant 4.

Spiritual care providers must be able to assess spirituality and help people access their spiritual resources in the direction of healthy integration. They must be able to work with a normative framework, both psychological and theological (or a theologically neutral ethical-philosophical normativity) while engaging care receivers on their own terms, especially when the care receivers' normative frameworks are deemed problematic or totally opposed to their own. Competent caregivers will normally find creative ways to make available safe and sacred spaces for care and healing to happen regardless of ideological incompatibility. It is therefore essential for them to be clear and consistent regarding their frames of reference and values while remaining open to challenge and correction by care receivers and colleagues alike.

The next section has an evaluation of fundamentalism in light of the framework and model outlined above. It demonstrates the nature of its toxicity and harm to the human spirit while also pointing to the way forward for transformation and healing.

FEATURES OF FUNDAMENTALIST SPIRITUALITY

Not all toxic spirituality is fundamentalist, strictly speaking.[24] However, all kinds of fundamentalism engender and sustain some measure of toxic spirituality. This section explores the essential structure and content of fundamentalism in terms of epistemology, ethics, and politics. We will thus illumine the claim that fundamentalism can cause irreparable damage and even death because it gravely impairs the human spirit. The case of Jim Jones and the Peoples Temple supplies an extreme but clear illustration that can be represented with another diagram, offering a model of human spirit as it relates to the spiritual dimensions of meaning, relatedness, and purpose.

---

24. For instance, a geographically and socioculturally isolated religious community that focuses on self-sufficient survival can generate spiritual toxicity without engaging in aggressive proselytism. It may be argued that such is the case of many Amish communities that combine Jesus-focused biblical literalism, culturally non-conformed segregation, and an internally enforced ethic. See Kraybill et al., *Amish Grace;* and *The Amish Way.* On the Amish and fundamentalism see also Hood Jr. et al., *Psychology of Religious Fundamentalism,* 133–54.

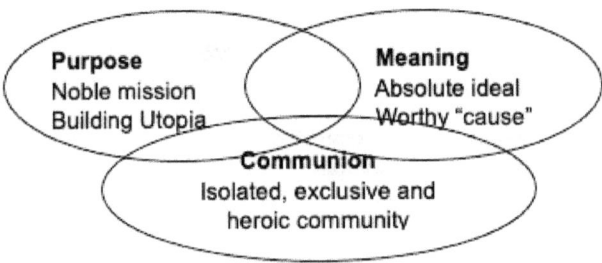

A model of the spirit applied to People's Temple spirituality.

This model can help us understand the challenge of fundamentalism by identifying three interrelated collapses that serve to negatively define fundamentalism—collapse of meaning, collapse of communion, and collapse of purpose. The *collapse of meaning* can be characterized in terms of *dogmatism* as an epistemological structure with recognizable features: absolute certainty regarding "fundamental" normative convictions; suppression of curiosity and questioning; eclipse of imagination and creativity; underestimation of mystery; incapacity to deal with paradox; and so on. Such collapse defines the epistemological failure of fundamentalism. Thus, we can claim that, in its religious and political expressions, fundamentalisms foster a caricature of *faith*.

The *collapse of communion* can be characterized in terms of *sectarianism*. Religious and other types of fundamentalism include the pretense of moral integrity/purity of those groups self-defined and identified by the corresponding ideological dogmatism. The kind of communion that fundamentalism promotes is necessarily exclusive and excluding; those who do not fit or accommodate become "strangers," adversaries, or even enemies. Such collapse of communion reveals personal as well as social, ethical, and moral failure. Therefore, we can assert that fundamentalism fosters a caricature of *love*.

The *collapse of purpose* can be characterized in terms of *proselytism*—of crusade-like attempts to create and distribute a radical politics based on the illusion of a certain, assured time to come. According to fundamentalist ideologies, the future is pre-determined; they thus offer a pseudo-utopian vision of a life project necessary to proclaim in order to persuade or "convert" the outsiders, and to defend that project by the most effective means possible. Such collapse reveals fundamentalism's political failure. Therefore, we can also claim that fundamentalism fosters a caricature of *hope*.

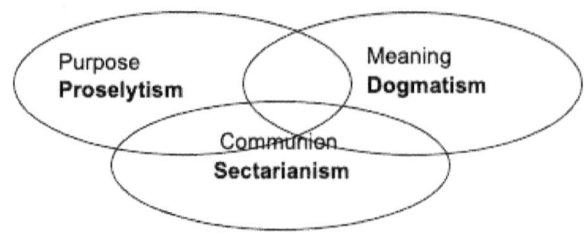

A model of the spirit applied to fundamentalist religion and spirituality.

Our study of spiritual toxicity also reveals a remarkable analogy between religious fundamentalisms and political authoritarian ideology and politics. The next section discusses the latter with focus on a major feature of the current sociocultural reality in the United States.

POLITICAL-SPIRITUAL TOXICITY: CHRISTIAN NATIONALISM AND WHITE SUPREMACY

At the time of this writing, there is a major concern in the United States—articulated from diverse perspectives, including spiritual healthcare and theology—regarding the growing political power of Christian nationalism connected to a white supremacy ideology. Several authors help us to understand the nature of this spreading cancer within the sociocultural landscape and its threat to democracy. A sample of their contributions is summarized below.

Christian nationalism is defined as "a cultural framework—a collection of myths, traditions, symbols, narratives and value systems—that idealizes and advocates a fusion of Christianity with American civil life."[25] In addition to debunking the myth that the United States was founded as a Christian nation,[26] scholars discuss the rise of religious fundamentalism in the country and its impact on politics,[27] and the special role of corporations and big business in promoting Christian nationalism.[28] A number of historians, social scientists, and theologians offer further insight and

---

25. Whitehead and Perry, *Taking America Back for God*, 10.

26. See Gorski and Perry, *Flag and the Cross*; Kruse and Zelizer, *Myth America*; and Seidel, *Founding Myth*.

27. See Keddie, *Republican Jesus*; Stewart, *Power Worshippers*.

28. See Kruse, *One Nation Under God*.

critique of key issues such as the embrace of right-wing extremism[29] and the betrayal of Christian faith,[30] particularly the relationship between white evangelicalism and masculinity in United States politics.[31]

Pamela Cooper-White addresses the formidable challenge of Christian nationalism from her position as both a psychotherapist and pastoral theologian. Of special interest for us is her analysis of the conscious and unconscious motivations of people drawn in by extremist beliefs. Among conscious motivations, she says, are the need for belonging and a sense of purpose; fear of loss of white social status and accompanying resentment; fear of loss of patriarchal power; and the irrational allure of conspiracy theories.[32] With psychoanalytic lenses, Cooper-White addresses the question of unconscious lures in terms of group dynamics, and in particular the magnetism of groupthink. She highlights the unconscious mental processes of *idealization* of and *identification* with a leader's character and aims—as can be seen most starkly in the cult-like symbiotic relationship between Donald Trump and his followers. The extreme cultural-political polarization and violence connected with Trump's stated views, verbal and texted statements, and politics are remarkable.

The Case of Donald Trump.

Two collections of essays thoroughly discuss the spiritual and political toxicity associated with the former president's leadership—including his relentless mendacity, demonization of opponents and support for violence against them, and embrace of extremist ideologies and authoritarian policies. First, before the 2020 presidential election in the United States, a group of thirty-seven psychiatrists and other mental health experts published a book offering detailed clinical observations of Trump's behavior, including his public speech, during his 2016 political campaign and resulting four-year presidency.[33] Significantly, they identified personality traits consistent

---

29. See Onishi, *Preparing for War*; Alberta, *Kingdom, the Power, and the Glory*; and Hendricks, *Christians Against Christianity*.

30. See Alberta, *Kingdom, the Power, and the Glory*; Hendricks, *Christians Against Christianity*; and Whitehead, *American Idolatry*.

31. See Kobes Du Mez, *Jesus and John Wayne*.

32. Cooper-White, *Psychology of Christian Nationalism*, 39–99.

33. Lee, *Dangerous Case of Donald Trump*. This case study remains especially relevant as Trump has continued to act in the same manner after his term in office was completed.

with "malignant narcissism"[34] as a possible combination of psychiatrically assessable disorders. They also describe Trump's "case" as demonstrating a harmful triangle of destructive leadership, susceptible followers, and conducive environments.

Another major publication addresses toxic spirituality both narrowly and broadly in its multiple critiques of the evangelical movement's embrace of Donald Trump's leadership and his policies.[35] The essays focus on issues of personal and social ethics and theological, historical, and constitutional issues related to the ideology and the movement he espouses. Of special interest for us are the views on both spiritual toxicity and, by contrast, wholesome moral character. In other words, the challenge is to reconsider normative features of desirable leadership and, more generally, healthy spirituality.

The political-spiritual toxicity generated by Christian nationalism and white supremacy in the United States—and often strongly linked to charismatic leadership, as we have just seen—can next be reframed in light of the notions of spirit and spirituality offered in this book. The emerging picture reveals a dangerous spiritual-political decline in the virtues of truth, grace, and justice, as represented in the following graphic.

---

34. Lee, *Dangerous Case of Donald* Trump, 46–63, 78–103. Malignant narcissism is not formally recognized as a diagnosis in the fifth edition of the American Psychiatric Association's *Diagnostic and Statistical Manual of Mental Disorders*. Nevertheless, I agree with these authors' characterization of "malignant narcissism" as blending traits of Narcissist Personality Disorder [DSM–5 301.81 (F60.81)] and Antisocial Personality Disorder [DSM–5 301.7 (F60.2)]. These traits are readily identifiable in Donald Trump's public behavior: an inflated sense of self-worth and grandiose logic of self-importance; a fixation with fantasies of endless success, control, and brilliance together with a constant need for admiration; a sense of entitlement; impulsive, reckless behavior; and a disregard for others borne of an empathy deficit. Such individuals often experience paranoid-like feelings and a sense of being treated unfairly, threatened or persecuted, and are aggressive, manipulative, and abusive without remorse.

35. Sider, *Spiritual Danger of Donald Trump*.

Spiritual Distress

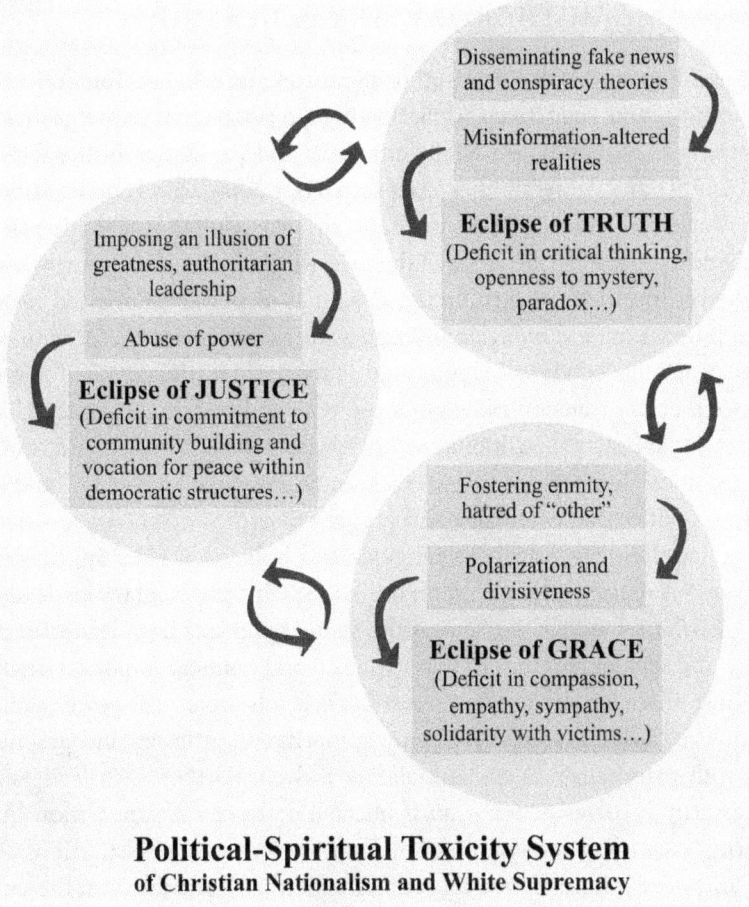

Political-Spiritual Toxicity System
of Christian Nationalism and White Supremacy

Key features of political-spiritual decline.

Similar toxicity can also easily be seen in previous and current political movements worldwide characterized by authoritarian leadership and anti-democratic ideology and politics. In all cases the defining feature is abuse of power, which pastoral theologians identify as a manifestation of evil.[36] Furthermore, common leadership traits are characteristic of both religious fundamentalist and political authoritarian leadership.

36. Poling, *Deliver Us from Evil*; Doehring, *Practice of Pastoral Care*, 104–13. Lust for power, narcissistic self-aggrandizement, and mendacity are key character traits described in Peck, *People of the Lie*, 69–84; 176–78. As far as sacred text characterizations are concerned, in the case of the New Testament, personalized manifestations of evil

TRAITS OF FUNDAMENTALIST AND AUTHORITARIAN LEADERSHIP

It is well known that political authoritarianism and religious fundamentalism can become seductive and fascinating alternatives for entire groups of people.[37] They may be especially attractive and persuasive in the face of ambiguities and vulnerabilities exacerbated by times of crisis and transition. But what defines the leaders that are able to successfully ensnare others into such closed systems? To answer this, we will integrate the contributions of Pierre Bourdieu concerning the dynamics of power manifested in human interaction and *mauvaise reconnaissance* (misrecognition)[38] with our already articulated views of human spirit and toxic spirituality. In doing so, we see that key traits of leaders that promote and sustain fundamentalism are: (a) unappealable positional authority that is both admired and feared; (b) technical competence as a special, unquestionable knowledge; and (c) radical politics that determine and propel mission. We can retrospectively recognize these traits in both religious and political leadership; they are also always present among certain militant groups and military leadership.

Positional authority refers to the status necessary for a leader to develop and sustain religious fundamentalism and political authoritarianism. In short, these leaders wield *power over* their followers. This power can be manifested not only through openly authoritarian attitudes and practices but with paternalism and manipulation as well. Further, such leadership necessarily involves *power against* internal and external opposition. Authority is assumed and conferred by both the represented institutions and the followers; it is not appealable but rather admired and feared at the same time. This leadership promotes a sense of solidarity within a community whose borders remain clearly defined and zealously defended.

Competence of knowledge, in the twofold sense of knowing and practical action (knowing how), is the second key trait of this leadership. Leaders

---

(Devil, Satan, "tempter," "adversary") are associated with temptation to wrongdoing or inaction, deception, divisiveness, and abuse of power (e.g., Matt 4:3–11; John 8:44; Acts 5:3; 1 Cor 7:5; Eph 6:11; 1 Pet 5:8–9).

37. At the time of this writing, fundamentalist religion—Christian, Islamic, Hindu, and Buddhist—is dangerously connected with political power in diverse countries such as the United States, Iran, India, and Myanmar, respectively. These forms of fundamentalism usually inspire and support violent extremism.

38. Bourdieu, *Outline of a Theory*, 168. In this theory, misrecognition denotes a false, imaginary, or incorrect understanding of the social world.

function according to fundamentalism's epistemological-ethical-political structure; they claim (and sometimes demonstrate) a seemingly superior, essential, and unquestionable knowing regarding the nature of reality. Often this involves a specific interpretation and application of the sacred texts that define the philosophic, religious, or political ideology of fundamentalism.[39] Obviously, this core competence correlates with the collapse of meaning (e.g., dogmatism, conspiracy theories) mentioned above.

Radical politics that determine and propel mission is the third key trait in this model. The logic of all forms of religious fundamentalism and political authoritarianism necessarily leads to some kind of "missional" project. The leadership that fundamentalism calls for must articulate a certain (pseudo)utopian vision of an alternative reality—a better world in the midst of or beyond history. It must stimulate vocation in service to such a dream, together with a program that promises or even guarantees its future realization. This is particularly, though not exclusively, the case of religious fundamentalism-political authoritarianism in its Christian and Islamist versions. It is imperative—in their thinking—that they recruit and indoctrinate faithful followers in order to carry out the mission.

Eventually, a number of followers of fundamentalist and authoritarian leaders might experience spiritual and moral struggles directly connected with their participation in the religious, political, and/or armed movement. Some followers and militants might develop moral injuries requiring special care.

UNDERSTANDING SPIRITUAL STRUGGLES AND MORAL INJURIES

Three general observations pertain to the content of this section. One is that *spiritual* and *moral* dimensions cannot be easily separated when dealing with struggles and injuries in spiritual care. Our preference is to keep them explicitly integrated in all cases without exception. Furthermore, these two sets of existential and caregiving challenges are universal and have been addressed for millennia across religious and other traditions, as

39. It is interesting that some philosophical and scientific associations, such as Marxist and Freudian psychoanalytic societies, can also develop fundamentalist tendencies concerning "orthodox" knowledge, exclusive membership, and assertive participation in the battle of ideas. This is ironic considering Marx and Freud themselves—great masters of suspicion, as Paul Ricoeur would call them—created valuable resources to unveil, analyze, and critique religious and other forms of fundamentalism!

documented in the sacred texts of all religious traditions. Finally, it should be noted that extensive research demonstrates the function of "spiritual-religious orienting systems"[40] in the prevention, processing, and positive or negative outcomes of both spiritual struggles and moral injuries.

Spiritual Struggles

A brief presentation of the concept of spiritual struggles follows closely the significant contribution of Ken Pargament, Julie Exline, and their associates. They have done comprehensive and systematic research explicitly from the perspective of the psychology of religion and spirituality.[41] The next paragraphs give a succinct review of that contribution, plus a few suggestions to enhance it.

First, spiritual struggles—existential distress, tension, conflict, and disorientation—must be considered as normal human experiences rather than symptoms of psychopathology or spiritual immaturity. Times of major transitions and life events, loss, abuse and other traumatic situations, and accumulated stressors all tend to be associated with higher levels of spiritual struggle. Research also shows a strong association between spiritual struggles and poor mental health; psychological problems can cause spiritual struggles such as depression, and spiritual despair can make a person experience depression.

Second, spiritual struggles are pervasive within our ongoing spiritual journeys. They are painful because they shake and shatter fundamental beliefs, values, practices, and relationships. And they are pivotal in that they open opportunities for spiritual growth. Research suggests that three categories of spiritual struggle can be found among people of all cultural and religious traditions in diverse social contexts: *supernatural* struggles

---

40. *Spiritual/religious orienting systems* are relatively stable patterns of belief, emotion, value, practice, and relationship that guide us along our preferred life journey to significant destinations. They can be viewed as philosophies of life or lived and intentional theologies. Doehring, *Practice of Pastoral Care*, 89–102, 191. Their functionality can be assessed psychologically in terms of normative criteria such as breadth and depth (capacity to see and approach life in its fullness); life affirmation (life infused with compassion, hope, support, and qualities such as strength, resources, competence, virtues, benevolence, gratitude, patience, and kindness); and cohesiveness (the degree to which someone's life journey is well-organized). See Pargament and Exline, *Working with Spiritual Struggles*, 104–33.

41. Pargament, *Spiritually Integrated Psychotherapy*; Pargament and Exline, *Working with Spiritual Struggles*; and Pargament and Exline, "Shaken to the Core."

(e.g., feeling abandoned or punished by God, angry with God, or tempted or tormented by demonic or evil entities); *intrapsychic* struggles (e.g., inner conflict related to meaning and doubt, sense of worth or purpose, shame and guilt); and *interpersonal* struggles (e.g., tension and conflicts with family, friends, faith communities, or clergy).

Third, spiritual struggles can lead to growth and wholeness, or decline and brokenness—or some combination thereof. Several factors have been identified regarding the trajectory of spiritual struggles toward existential reorientation: openness to change and willingness to face and process, rather than avoid, those struggles; an ability to reframe them within a larger benevolent spiritual perspective; the experience of sacred moments that offset the effects of spiritual struggles; capacity to make meaning out of the struggle; and availability of support experienced in the midst of the struggle.[42] In light of the model of spirit and spirituality presented in chapter 2, to the stated goal of searching for meaning and significance underscored in the study by Pargament and Exline, we add the longings for communion-connectedness and for vocational purpose.

Fourth, adequately addressing spiritual struggles in caregiving situations starts with implicit and explicit psycho-spiritual assessment in a context of rapport and connectedness. The "pattern of wise discernment" described in chapter 3 can serve as a strengthened overarching framework for the caregiving process. Furthermore, strategies for negotiating religious difference (chapter 5) are necessary to minimize the risks of misunderstanding and subsequent aggression—especially, though not exclusively, in interfaith caregiving situations. Specific research also highlights the importance of normalizing spiritual struggles by naming, reassuring, and facilitating acceptance; and by encouraging spiritual reflection while also helping to access resources connected with care receivers' diverse wisdom traditions.[43]

These contributions from a psychology of religion and spirituality are necessary and indeed indispensable for all groups of spiritual care practitioners and theoreticians. At the same time, as consistently proposed in this book, theological material can enhance both the understanding of, as well as clinical work with spiritual struggles, as illustrated in Asma's case. Therefore, further interdisciplinary research in this area should include

---

42. Pargament and Exline, "Shaken to the Core," 125.

43. Pargament and Exline, *Working with Spiritual Struggles*, 137–61. See also Jones, *Spirit in Session*, 112–34.

systematic, comparative, in-depth studies across religious-theological and other philosophical views undergirding wisdom traditions. Of course, such observation also applies to the focus on moral injuries as a distinct category.

Moral Injuries

Research on moral injury has developed separately from the focus on spiritual struggles summarized above (which includes moral struggle[44] as one of the types). As a study focus it was associated first with the experiences of military veterans returning to the United States from Vietnam and Middle East wars. The next paragraphs summarize main findings and ramifications, starting with the special situation of moral injury in the military.

Military moral injury continues to be a focal concern among chaplains and war veterans and their families.[45] In the United States and elsewhere, military chaplains are officers within the hierarchical military structure. They must provide combat stress support, advise commanders on religious and moral matters, and offer care and counseling for service members and others. Their caregiving work includes the prevention of moral injury by strengthening soldiers' preparedness to participate in a given military mission, which assumes unwavering support of such mission.[46] Secondary and tertiary prevention[47] can take place as timely intervention and programmed

---

44. In the work of Pargament and Exline, "moral struggle" is included within the intrapersonal category of "spiritual struggles" (characterized as taking the form of tensions and guilt about not living up to one's higher standards and wrestling with attempts to follow moral principles). They point out that "moral injury" studies have focused on the downside of spiritual struggles and question the cross-sectional nature of moral injury research. *Working with Spiritual Struggles*, 246–48.

45. See Meagher and Pryer, *War and Moral Injury*; Ramsay and Doehring, *Military Moral Injury*; and Moon, *Warriors between Worlds*. These and other references included in this section assume that "moral injury" is not necessarily a psychological disorder such as clinically diagnosed PTSD (post-traumatic stress disorder), although these two categories of mental distress overlap in some ways (e.g., experience of anger, depression, anxiety, insomnia, nightmares). Moral injuries can happen apart from and as distinct from PTSD and include sorrow, grief, regret, shame, and a sense of alienation.

46. It might be especially challenging for chaplains to support the rationale and execution of so-called "wars of choice" (that is, crusades of sorts that don't fit "just war" criteria), not to mention the overwhelming devastation and presumed "collateral damage" always caused by war. Parenthetically, it must be added that military chaplains can also play a major role in keeping peace and supporting reconstruction work. See Moore, *Military Chaplains*.

47. As in previous chapters, we continue to apply the concepts of "primary,"

caregiving support for healing.[48] In any event, military chaplaincy in the United States must be considered within the overarching social-political context of a war culture that blends nationalism and militarization.[49]

As Rita Nakashima Brock asserts, since its inception the concept of moral injury has been intersectional and cross-disciplinary, with significant work appearing in the social sciences, classics, philosophy, religion, literature, and medicine.[50] Reflection on moral injury has been fluid and ongoing among military veterans, clinicians and counselors who work with them, psychologists, moral philosophers, theologians, pastors, and academics from diverse disciplines, among others.[51] A comprehensive definition includes both perpetration and betrayal: having done, failed to prevent, or been witness to actions that transgress moral values; and/or betrayal of what is right experienced as broken trust (e.g., action by comrades, a commander, or an abusive clergy person).[52] Simply put in the words of Larry Kent Graham, moral injury and even trauma can result from the moral dissonance and dilemma created "when we are unable to do what we believe is right, or when wrongs are done to us . . . [or] when doing the right thing results in harm to others and distress to ourselves, in spite of our intentions."[53]

Numerous contributions offer complementary caregiving guidelines for moral injury situations, beginning with those specifically fitting for war veterans: an evidence-based intercultural approach; accessible spiritual

"secondary," and "tertiary" prevention according to Caplan, *Principles of Preventive Psychiatry*.

48. See Brock and Lettini, *Soul Repair*; and Moon, *Coming Home*.

49. See Denton-Borhaug, *And Then Your Soul is Gone*; "Moral Injury;" and "'Like Acid Slipping.'" See also Meagher, *Killing from the Inside Out*. For the presentation of an extreme case of nationalism, racism, and war-culture, see Bergen, *Between God and Hitler*. During the Second World War, approximately one thousand Christian chaplains accompanied Wehrmacht forces wherever they went; they were witnesses to all sorts of atrocity and helped to normalize extreme violence and legitimate its perpetrators. Those military chaplains played a key role in propagating a narrative of righteousness that erased Germany's victims and transformed the aggressors into noble figures who suffered but triumphed over their foes. Bergen examines Protestant and Catholic military chaplains in Germany from Hitler's rise to power, to defeat, collapse, and Allied occupation. She offers insight into how Christian clergy loyally served the cause of genocide.

50. Brock, Prologue to *Bible and Moral Injury*, xi.

51. Kelle, *Moral Injury*, 8. See also Meagher and Pryer, *War and Moral Injury*.

52. Kelle, *Moral Injury*, 8–13.

53. Graham, *Moral Injury*, 97.

practices (e.g., deep listening, circle process, lamentation, consciousness examen); and storytelling, memorials, and rituals for recovery via cleansing, forgiveness, and restoration.[54] Together with counseling and psychotherapy for individuals, groups, and families, the support of welcoming faith and other communities is essential.[55]

We agree with Graham that the concept of moral injury ought to be expanded and placed in the context of everyday moral living of personal and communal moral discernment, action, healing, and recovery. For such overarching purpose, Graham proposes a four-dimensional collaborative process aimed at enhancing moral decisions and healing moral injuries: (a) naming the moral injury; (b) framing the moral injury in actionable terms; (c) enacting moral change; and (d) revising moral histories.[56] We add that this proposal can also be viewed as a form of spiritual-moral discernment aimed at engaging and strengthening moral-spiritual intelligence, as presented in chapter 3.

A final highlight has to do with the function of sacred texts[57] that can inform, inspire, and guide spiritual care in the face of moral injury. A clear example is the Jewish understanding of *Teshuvá* as a framework and patterned process for forgiveness and healing that must include: recognition of wrongdoing, remorse, confession, desisting from wrongdoing, and restitution as is possible.[58] Illustrations can also be taken from sacred texts in situations where both care seekers and caregivers are familiar with pertinent material. Teachings, poetry and prayers (e.g., confession, lament), and stories can thus be helpful in both intra faith and inter-faith situations.[59] There is also the case where sacred texts might have been emotionally and spiritually injurious for care receivers and need to be reinterpreted, reframed, or even rejected. Finally, on a more theoretical level, interdisciplinary conversation with biblical scholars, religious studies specialists, and theologians

---

54. Ramsay and Doehring, *Military Moral Injury*, 20–54, 55–78, 142–68.

55. Moon, *Coming Home*.

56. Graham, *Moral Injury*, 78–79, 109–52.

57. The implicit function of sacred texts in connection with spiritual struggles and moral injuries can be further explored within the study of their place in religious wisdom traditions, as discussed in the previous chapter.

58. Blumenthal, "Soul Repair," 37–39, 45–46.

59. The next chapter of this book presents several strategies and approaches to navigating religious difference in spiritual care.

can be mutually enriching,[60] especially when engaged with a commitment to liberation (e.g., decolonization), healing, and transformation.

VISUALIZING TRANSFORMATION

Transformation is the aspiration and goal of spiritual care in the face of religious fundamentalism and other forms of toxic spirituality, spiritual struggle, and moral injury. It is a process of systemic change in the lives of those who receive spiritual care. Thus, transformation is second-order change, as in "revolution" or radical change. Whereas a change within a given system is a "first-order change," systemic change is the change of the system as such. It is therefore fitting to apply this term to genuine personal conversion experiences, such as those of former members of fundamentalist religious groups.[61]

Transformation can be identified and appraised on intrapersonal, interpersonal, and community levels. In addition to what individual or group therapy can accomplish intra- and interpersonally, successful strategies and approaches confronting toxicity and distress can have a positive communal and social effect as well. This includes, of course, the potential transformation of religious communities and social-political movements.

Research demonstrates that authentic systemic changes can happen when, or to the extent that, interrelated outcomes are met: (a) contextual appropriation of new insights results in revelatory *meaning* and paradigm-perspective change; (b) the *experience* of community, solidarity, and integrity is enriched (e.g., a new sense of belonging and communion is birthed); and (c) empowerment and reorientation begins movement toward creative, liberating, or community-building *action* (e.g., devising healing and reconstruction strategies, reconciliation, and others).

In other words, transformation at the *existential* or *spiritual* level can be appreciated as a process that reshapes the human *spirit* as follows: (a) from deception, illusion, denial, and meaninglessness to a new vision and understanding in which "truth" is constructed and revealed afresh (a new "orthodoxy," theologically speaking, with critically held conviction and openness to mystery); (b) from isolation, exclusion, alienation, condemnation, division, and enmity to connectedness, communion, community,

---

60. See McDonald, *Exploring Moral Injury*; and Kelle, *Bible and Moral Injury*. These texts illustrate how moral injury theory can enrich sacred text hermeneutics and vice versa.

61. Schipani, "Fundamentalism as Toxic Spirituality," 181–87.

and solidarity (a new "orthopathy" or "orthokardia," in the case of religious faith); and (c) from misplaced vocation, inertia, resignation, disorientation, despair, and hopelessness to re-orientation and empowerment for justice and peace (a new "orthopraxis" and sense of purpose and life project). These existential or spiritual dimensions must be engaged as dynamically interrelated.

Empirical evidence is abundant, including countless personal testimonies[62] and those of disparate groups such as Fundamentalists Anonymous and veterans recovering from moral-spiritual injury after war. That evidence also confirms that dismantling and deconstructing psycho-spiritual and epistemological-ethical-political structures of fundamentalism and other forms of toxic spirituality, and of struggle and injury, require participation in communities of support and discernment. Without such enfolding accompaniment, people can quickly fall into vacuums of meaninglessness, self-condemning isolation, and self-destructive fatalism with the suppression of all life projects—as documented in the large percentage of war veterans that die by suicide.[63] An alternative is, of course, to move content-wise, so to speak, from one fundamentalism to another, but that cannot be considered as transforming change according to the criteria we have discussed.

In light of our views on human spirit, the following diagrams suggest that the "content" observable, for instance, in Islamist militant groups and all kinds of militaristic spirituality resembles what was highlighted concerning the story of the Peoples Temple.

---

62. See Feldman, *Unorthodox*; Phelps-Roper, *Unfollow*; and Nawaz, *Radical*.

63. Regular armed forces can be included among the groups that must operate with a closed, "fundamentalist" system and its characteristic structure in terms of ideology and leadership. Those military forces cannot function effectively unless its authoritarian leadership structure is consistently supported by military versions of dogmatism (nationalism, patriotism), sectarianism (good people clearly separated from and against evil people), and mission (heroic vocation to destroy "evil" in specific ways). Nevertheless, it must be clear that in no way do we posit moral equivalence between, say, radical Islamist or white supremacist militias and regular armed forces.

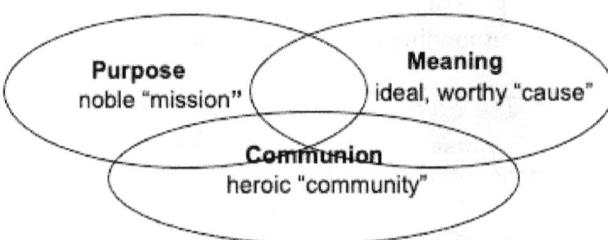

Application of the model to religious and political extremism
and militaristic spiritualities.

The training and indoctrination necessary to sustain such spiritual configuration must include the goal of fostering in the recruits and followers the appropriation of fundamentalist ideology and values, and development of certain competencies in integrated and integrating ways. In other words, recruits and followers must conform to the system along the lines represented below.[64]

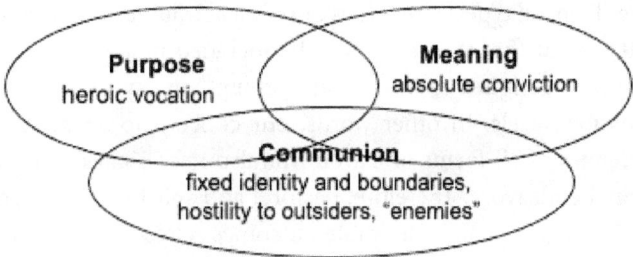

Spiritual features of cult followers and recruits *before* the collapse of the toxic system.

Clinical and other studies demonstrate that, when the toxic system is no longer viable, for example in the face of the atrocities witnessed or perpetrated in combat, a major and potentially traumatic disruption takes place. This is the condition identifiable in the studies of, and approaches to, both the "religious trauma syndrome" and "moral and spiritual injury."

64. Military training, by design, destabilizes and diminishes the constancy of recruits' preexistent moral orienting systems. The training strips away these moral codings, including values, beliefs, behaviors, and meaningful relationships. Recruitment programs indoctrinate recruits with a new moral orienting system that supports functioning in military contexts and the high-stress environments of combat. Doehring, "Military Moral Injury," 22–23.

These syndromes present multidimensional faces of spiritual or existential anxiety.[65] The corresponding representation follows.

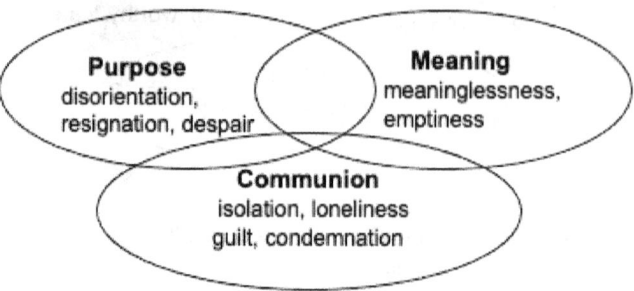

Spiritual features of cult followers and war veterans *after* the collapse of the toxic system.

Our study suggests that the goals of transformation must be articulated as psycho-spiritual reorientation, that is, as systemic change at the spiritual or existential level as described above. These goals pertain especially in secondary and tertiary prevention while caring for people needing to recover from all types of religious or political trauma and moral-spiritual injury. It is clear that they must also be included in any primary prevention approach designed to nurture and strengthen psycho-spiritual health at all possible levels. In other words, our concern to effectively address the challenges of all forms of extremism also necessitates comprehensive educational endeavors. Therefore, pastoral and spiritual caregivers as well as educators can visualize desirable outcomes related to the fundamental questions of meaning, communion, and purpose as suggested below.

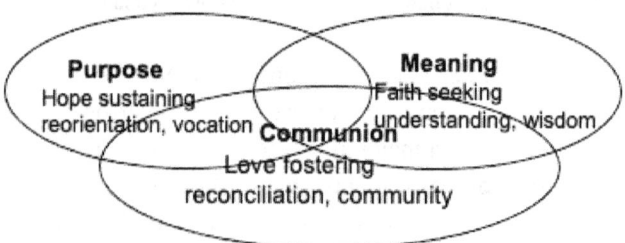

Desirable outcomes of spiritual or existential transformation.

65. As indicated in chapter 1, theologian Paul Tillich insightfully identified and described main features of existential anxiety in terms of the threefold threat of nonbeing—emptiness, condemnation, and annihilation. Tillich, *Courage to Be*, 32–77.

Regardless of conceptualization specifics, spiritual care receivers and caregivers collaborate in the search for recovering unique versions of healthy spirituality. The focus of the next chapter has to do with *method*— that is, the way toward that goal. Given the overarching purpose of this book, the chosen framework is religious difference in caregiving situations.

5

Strategies and Approaches in Interfaith Spiritual Care

ELSEWHERE IN THIS BOOK are references to unfolding research and new publications on interreligious care in the face of increased global pluralization during the last two decades. Representatives of diverse traditions are adding substantially to the pioneering work of Christian clinicians and theoreticians. This chapter addresses one of the key challenges and opportunities associated with multifaith contexts: the methodological and clinical question of how spiritual caregivers can effectively engage significant *difference* in intercultural and interreligious caregiving situations. Simply stated, the twofold goal is to understand and foster competent practice by counselors, psychotherapists, chaplains, pastors, and other spiritual caregivers.

 We will start with a story from a sacred text that illustrates the difficulty often present when unexpectedly encountering a multiply *different other.* That introductory vignette is followed by "timely consultation" and "opportune referral" as strategies to employ under certain circumstances. Next is the section on "bridge-building strategies," with specific ways caregivers and care receivers can creatively cooperate in the therapeutic process; it is divided into the categories of "seeking common ground" and "collaborative accommodation." Then follows a discussion of "code switching" as a resource employed at the caregivers' discretion. Case studies illustrate the nature of those strategies and approaches and illumine pertinent issues of competence in interfaith spiritual care. The final section of the chapter has a repertoire of caregiving methods and techniques typical of, but not restricted to, counseling for the purpose of facilitating spiritual reflection.

A PARADIGMATIC STORY: STRUGGLE TO CARE IN THE FACE OF DIFFERENCE

> Jesus left that place and went away to the district of Tyre and Sidon. Just then a Canaanite woman from that region came out and started shouting, "Have mercy on me, Lord, Son of David; my daughter is tormented by a demon." But he did not answer her at all. And his disciples came and urged him, saying, "Send her away, for she keeps shouting after us." He answered, "I was sent only to the lost sheep of the house of Israel." But she came and knelt before him, saying, "Lord, help me." He answered, "It is not fair to take the children's food and throw it to the dogs." She said, "Yes, Lord, yet even the dogs eat the crumbs that fall from their masters' table." Then Jesus answered her, "Woman, great is your faith! Let it be done for you as you wish." And her daughter was healed from that moment.[1]

The most striking part of the story is Jesus's initial response to the request of the woman: first a deafening silence, then an uncharacteristic affirmation of ethnic boundaries, followed by parabolic refusal. At that moment he appears to regard the woman's request as inappropriate—even as outrageously out of place. Only in this particular Gospel story does Jesus ignore a supplicant, place the barrier of ethnicity before a plea for help, and then use offensive language to reiterate the barrier. The Canaanite woman understands the grave implications of Jesus's initial response, but she proceeds wisely and daringly to reframe and recast it.

Jesus's original challenge to the woman merely restates the status quo of gender, ethnic, cultural, religious, and political divisions. Her counter-challenge calls him to look to the place of new possibilities across and beyond the established boundaries. Instead of accepting the dichotomy of children (insiders who receive food) versus dogs (outsiders who get no food), she imagines that both the children and the dogs can be graciously fed inside, within the same household and from the same table.

The sacred text implies that multiple kinds of "stretching" are happening—those of geographic, ethnic, gender, religious, theological, sociocultural, moral, and political dimensions. No wonder, then, that the intrusion

---

1. Matt 15:21–28. This account adds significant details to the story as found in Mark 7:24–30. See also Schipani, "Biblical Foundations," 51–67. In addition to exemplary accounts such as Luke 24:13–35 (included in chapter 3 of this book as a paradigmatic story of companioning in the face of loss), stories of conflict and ambivalence in sacred writings can also instruct, inspire, and guide interfaith spiritual caregivers.

of the woman into his life and sense of vocation stunned Jesus. Because this narrative has much spatial and contextual import, it is significant that this marginal Canaanite woman emerges as the center of the story; in fact, it is primarily her story.

We observe a surprisingly transformative reversal: Jesus comes to acknowledge that she has *great* faith. His praise at the end suggests that, in this encounter in the borderlands, the Canaanite woman has become a kind of prophetic and wise teacher. Out of her desire for her daughter's healing, she has acted and spoken counterculturally and counter-politically. She might have reminded Jesus of the larger vision of a divine commonwealth of care and justice.

We can assume that Jesus would have been socialized into the conventional wisdom of his time and dominant culture. According to such socialization as a first-century Jew, prudence involved keeping clear boundaries; adhering to certain criteria of what is proper, clean, normal, and appropriate; and holding to right categories and patterns of perception, thought, and relationships. Then an outsider, a multiply marginal person, challenges Jesus to relate and care across and beyond those boundaries. She gives him an opportunity to respond in tune with an alternative wisdom, expressed in an ethic and politic of compassion and radical inclusiveness. Jesus faces a major conflict and temptation from within, so to speak, and eventually he chooses wisely after being creatively challenged by the foreign woman.

The story of the Canaanite woman points to the possibility of undermining and dismantling that is, dialectically speaking, to negate the negation imposed by—*chosenness* as ideology, as justification for excluding and discriminating against the other, the stranger, the foreigner, the "pagan." A powerful paradox is at work here. At least three possible applications for caregiving can be drawn from this story.

First, "borderlands"—contextual dislocations, unfamiliar places where we encounter significant difference—can become privileged spaces for transformative care. Places of vulnerability and marginality, in particular, are potentially epiphanic or revelatory; that is, they can be sources of surprising insight and new meaning. Second, situations of conflict—especially those of resistance meeting counter-resistance—can open transformative opportunities for both care seekers and caregivers. Finally, despite the inherently asymmetrical nature of caregiving relationships, and of interfaith care in particular, creative collaboration can result in growth, liberation, and healing for both care seekers and caregivers.

Unexpected encounters with significant difference can be very challenging, and especially so in interfaith situations. Therefore, caregivers must appropriate strategies that help to make therapeutic communication possible and effective. That is material offered in the sections that follow.

CONSULTATION AND REFERRAL

It is commonplace to assume that caregivers of any kind must commit themselves to the basic principle, "First, do no harm," a popular saying that derives from the Latin phrase, *primum non nocere* or *primum nil nocere*. Of course, any form of clinical malpractice must always be avoided! Hence, given the potential for misunderstanding and verbal and emotional-spiritual violence particularly inherent in interfaith care situations, it is fitting to first discuss consultation and referral as appropriate and, indeed, indispensable strategies. Competencies such as cultural humility, contemplative and reverent curiosity, emotional-interpersonal intelligence, and ongoing self-reflexivity, are among the key components of such necessary competence.

Consultation with others is normally necessary before and often during interfaith caregiving. In addition to bibliographic and other resources available,[2] there is the wisdom of trusted colleagues with interfaith expertise and experience, whether or not they represent the tradition of care receivers. Thomas Plante's thorough discussion of consultation in psychotherapy applies to other forms of spiritual care as well.[3] And, of course, caregivers themselves are the primary source of guidance from the start of the caregiving process. Therefore, consultation can be viewed as a strategy of *primary prevention* of harm, that is, before the caregiving encounter takes place and during the first steps of the caregiving relationship.

Consultation can also play a role as a strategy of *secondary prevention*, when an assessment of forward movement in the caregiving process reveals the need for course correction. In this situation, caregivers must reorient their work with the kinds of resources mentioned above, as well as with their own life expertise. Kathleen Greider reminds us that meeting constructively and creatively amid difference always encourages *power sharing*: "It is entirely appropriate to ask clients about their religious location(s),

---

2. See (for psychotherapists) Richards and Bergin, *Handbook of Psychotherapy*; (for counselors) Sue et al., *Counseling the Culturally Diverse*; and (for chaplains) Wintz and Handzo, *Handbook*.

3. Plante, *Spiritual Practices in Psychotherapy*, 131–45.

stating explicitly our desire to know about their tradition from their point of view."[4] Greider astutely labels this a "teach me" approach—"a 'perspective shift' during which counselors [or chaplains or psychotherapists] make themselves students of their clients' religious knowledge and experience."[5] Furthermore, the caregiver's willingness to yield power by learning from the care receiver seems certain to have connective and therapeutic value.

Referral can also be seen as an interfaith care strategy of either primary, secondary, or even *tertiary prevention*.[6] For example, referral to a different caregiver of their same religious or spiritual tradition can often be requested by hospital patients, incarcerated people, or their families even before a caregiving relationship begins. Referral can also be recommended or decided by the caregiver; in fact, competent counselors and psychotherapists will always be "sensitive to circumstances (e.g., personal biases, value conflicts, lack of knowledge of the clients' religious tradition) that could dictate referral of a religious client to a member of his or her religious tradition."[7] In other situations, referral may not involve the termination of a caregiving relationship, such as when care receivers are advised to *additionally* consult with clergy or other authorities in their tradition. In any of these events, as Martin Walton notes, caregivers do well to always respect difference, while making sure not to exaggerate or absolutize it by assuming that peoples of different cultures differ from each other essentially.[8]

In this vein, we now proceed to discussing interfaith caregiving engagement that explicitly acknowledges difference. The sections that follow provide a response to the question of method(s): How can we actually approach and navigate the therapeutic process in interfaith situations?

BRIDGE-BUILDING STRATEGIES

Whether it's called *therapeutic alliance* (namely in counseling and psychotherapy) or, more generally, the *caregiving relationship*, a collaborative connection between care receiver and caregiver is always essential. Together they identify needs and resources, desirable outcomes, and fitting

---

4. Greider, "Religious Location and Counseling," 47.
5. Greider, "Religious Location and Counseling," 47.
6. See Caplan, *Principles of Preventive Psychiatry*.
7. Richards and Bergin, *Handbook of Psychotherapy*, 13. See also Clinebell, *Basic Types of Pastoral Care*, 393–412.
8. Walton, "Encountering Difference," 56.

approaches or interventions. However, creating and maintaining such a bond can be particularly challenging in the face of perceived major difference. Our analysis of empirical evidence in multiple cultural contexts and institutional settings finds at least three kinds of bridge-building strategies at work in interfaith spiritual care. (This bridge-building metaphor intentionally links the experience of *difference* with interpersonal and intersubjective *distance* as analogy; and also with finding common *ground* or *space* as necessary therapeutic context.) Those sets of strategies are characterized as (a) seeking common ground;[9] (b) collaborative accommodation; and (c) caregiver code switching.

Seeking Common Ground

Chapters 2 and 3 offered theoretical background and clinical support for attempting to minimize difference in intercultural and interfaith caregiving situations. Two fundamental claims were thoroughly discussed: the universal or transcultural nature of the human spirit and the enduring significance and value of religious and non-religious wisdom traditions. In a nutshell, the human spirit longs for wisdom in its search for meaning, communion, and purpose; wisdom traditions address that search across cultures. At its best, interfaith care connects wisdom traditions with the longings of the human spirit in socioculturally and otherwise contextually pertinent ways. Brief case studies in the following paragraphs illustrate how care seekers and caregivers can find common ground in healthcare centers. The focus of the two cases selected is the question of offered or requested prayer[10] in interfaith situations involving Christian chaplains.[11]

---

9. Notice that we choose the phrase "seeking common ground" instead of the term "neutralizing"; the latter is commonly used by sociologists in reference to minimizing the significance of cultural differences or accentuating common perspectives in meaning making. See Cadge and Sigalow, "Negotiating Religious Differences."

10. Chaplains and other pastoral and spiritual caregivers possess a unique repertoire of interventions, prayer being chief among them. By now it should be obvious that quality pastoral and spiritual care requires the capacity to make available both formal and informal prayers for persons of all faiths. Further, it is evident that they should exercise strong social-emotional intelligence to cautiously interpret the care receivers' cues and to assess their comfort level. Therefore, interfaith caregivers should equip themselves with a variety of resources and skills to facilitate the delicate connection between care receivers and what is sacred or holy for them.

11. The following case illustrations are composites of actual case studies collected during the last several years. For earlier versions of the case studies, see Bueckert and

Spiritual Care in our Multifaith World

A Baptist Chaplain Cares for a Jewish Family

It was Saturday evening when Chaplain Bill's pager contact informed him of a need at a palliative care unit. When Bill arrived, he found the patient's room filled with family members, the young men among them wearing yarmulkes (skullcaps). A woman with gray hair was standing by the bed; Bill soon realized that she was the wife of the dying man. He introduced himself and she said, "Pastor, thank you for coming. Jacob is not going to make it, and we appreciate that you are here."

Not that there was much doubt, but the chaplain confirmed with the family that they were Jewish and then asked them if it would be helpful if he contacted a rabbi. Jacob's wife smiled and said, "No, our God is your God, and he hears our prayers." Bill affirmed her statement and then, since Jacob was not responsive, he asked the woman if Jacob had the assurance of God's love and care in those dying days. She smiled again and said, "Oh, yes, he knew."

Bill was then introduced to every person in the room, and Jacob's wife directed a grandson to get him a chair so that he could sit with her by the bed. Bill sat down and invited the people in the room to tell him about Jacob. Different individuals spoke up, telling him about their relationship and sharing something about how special Jacob was to them. There was laughter as family members remembered things that had happened or lessons they had learned. Forty minutes passed quickly, and when the time was appropriate, the chaplain stood and told them how special it was for Jacob and his wife to have a loving family present at such a time. He encouraged them to keep telling their stories and to tell Jacob how much he meant to them.

Bill usually concluded his visits with a prayer. He wanted to be sensitive to how he, a Baptist chaplain, could best minister to a Jewish family, so he asked them if he could leave them with a prayer and a blessing from the Bible. They agreed that would be good, so he read Psalm 23, offered a prayer, and then blessed them with the benediction from Deut 31:8: "It is the Lord who goes before you. He will be with you; he will not fail you or forsake you. Do not fear or be dismayed."

As he rode the elevator to the lobby, Bill was aware that he had just experienced a special moment unlike any he had ever experienced. He had been able to contribute to a meaningful grieving process with people whose

Schipani (2009), 25–45; 81–98.

religious experiences were similar and yet very different from his own. At the same time, he had been blessed by the Jewish family. It was affirming to know that being sensitive to the belief system that has given people hope through the years makes it possible to connect with them deeply and significantly.

This case study addresses the question of *core competencies* that meet established standards of excellence in interfaith spiritual care. It can be read as a threefold example of identifiable principles, or dependable guides, in terms of the *being, knowing,* and *doing* competencies introduced in chapter 1 and thoroughly discussed in the next chapter.[12]

A Mennonite Chaplain Encounters Two Hindu Men

Tarak was a forty-three-year-old Hindu man being treated on the neuromedical surgical unit following a stroke. Originally from India, he was currently living in the United States. Chaplain Leah had visited Tarak once before, and this time another man was with him standing at the foot of

---

12. First, Bill's ministry illustrates core competencies of *being* indispensable to full *presence* with the family:
- A clear sense of personal and vocational identity
- Optimal self-awareness, including a realistic view of strengths and limitations
- Character strengths such as acceptance, respect, and sensitivity; humility and compassion; freedom to be vulnerable and openness to new experiences; etc.
- A spirituality that embraces complexity and paradox (e.g., regarding the normativity of Jesus Christ and the truthfulness of the care receivers' Jewish faith)

Second, as a spiritual caregiver, Bill demonstrates the value of several core competencies of *knowing* essential for *understanding* and *discernment*:
- A philosophy of caregiving grounded in his Christian faith tradition and shaped by professional training and experience
- Knowledge of the complexities, dynamics, richness, and challenges of interfaith situations
- Understanding of at least one other faith tradition different than his own
- Clinical and theological knowing and assessment

Finally, Bill's work illustrates core competencies of *doing* required for the fine art of *companioning* in spiritual care:
- Relating to the Jewish family in ways that engage their emotions and spirituality
- Encouraging and guiding the family members in a time of storytelling
- Acting as a participant-observer who internally monitors ongoing caregiving activity, thus maximizing effectiveness while avoiding invasive or intrusive interventions
- Providing a number of responses in several caregiving modes (e.g., gently probing, supporting, praying, reading, blessing)

the bed. During their conversation Leah learned that this man was Tarak's friend Peter, also from India but having lived in the United States for a longer period of time. He was fluent in both Hindi and English.

"How have you been since the last time we talked?" Leah asked. Tarak's face displayed confusion. Leah tried again: "How are you?"

"Fine," he answered.

"Have you been doing exercises?" Leah inquired, trying to open a conversation that connected with the first time she had met him. Peter interpreted the question.

"Yes," Tarak answered. "In the mornings," Peter added.

"What kind of exercises do you do?" Peter again interpreted Leah's question. Tarak began to lift his left arm up and down with his right hand. Leah surmised: "Arm exercises. And walking?"

Peter answered, "He uses a walker, and somebody supports his left side."

Leah asked Peter, "Are you here when he does his exercises?"

"No, I'm not here in the morning."

"How did the two of you meet?" she asked him.

"We come from the same place in India, and we have the same last name."

"Oh, really? But you met in this area?"

"Yes. A friend of his is also my friend, and so we met. I am looking for a job and I heard that he was in the hospital. So I came here to be with him—I like to be here when he needs help."

Turning to Tarak, Leah said, "Good to have friends, isn't it?" Tarak nodded, and she continued. "Last time we talked, you told me that you are Hindu."

"Yes," Tarak replied.

"As a Christian, I'd love to know more about what it is like to be Hindu." Tarak smiled and nodded. "It must be different here," she added, "where there aren't very many people who are Hindu."

Peter responded: "In India about 80 percent are Hindu, 13 percent are Muslim, and the rest are Christian and others."

"Oh, I see," Leah said. "That must be a different experience."

"Yes, it's different," Peter replied. "But I go into a church."

"A Christian church?"

"Yes. There is one God. Whether I am in a temple or in a mosque or in a church—Krishna, Rama, Jesus—it's all the same God."

"Different names for one God," said Leah.

"Yes—different names for one God. That's what I believe."

"What about you?" Leah asked, looking at Tarak. Peter interpreted her question.

Pointing up with his finger, Tarak said, "One God."

"I also believe that," Leah stated. "Do you also pray in the Hindu tradition?"

Peter interpreted and then said, "Yes, we pray."

"What is it like for you to pray?"

Peter chuckled and interpreted. Tarak put his hands together and bowed his head.

"Do you know what he is saying?" Peter asked Leah. "He is saying when we go into the temple we stand in front of the god, we put our hands together—like you—and bow our head—the same. In a temple there is a statue, in a mosque there may be nothing, and in a Christian church there is a statue of Jesus. The method doesn't matter; it's what is in the heart that's important."

"Yes, God knows the heart," Leah replied. Looking at Tarak she asked, "What do you pray for?" Peter interpreted, and Tarak touched his arm, looking at Leah.

"For health, for the body to be restored," guessed Leah.

Peter added, "For strength in his leg and his arm so that he can go back to India."

"Yes, of course," Leah said. "To recover and be well again, to go home."

Peter returned to the subject of God. "Human is the same everywhere—one God. But not everyone believes that. If everyone believed that, the world would be very different, I think. Now there is always fighting."

Leah agreed. "Yes, it seems that our differences sometimes get in the way." Looking at Tarak, she asked, "Would it be all right if I say a prayer with you?"

Peter interpreted the question and then said, "That would be all right." He interpreted to Tarak as Leah prayed, line by line.

"Oh God, who loves us all, thank you for the opportunity to talk with Peter and Tarak. As Tarak spends these days in the hospital, we pray that your healing will strengthen his body and that your spirit of peace would bless him. Thank you for the friendship that Tarak and Peter share. Thank you for the care of the medical staff here. Give the staff guidance and wisdom. We pray that Tarak will regain his strength day by day. We pray that he will soon be able to return home to India. May Tarak know your love and healing through the care of those around him. Amen."

After exchanging a few more words, Leah thanked them for the visit, and they said goodbye.

Collaborative Accommodation

This caregiving strategy can also be viewed as a variation of seeking common ground. In this case, care seeker and caregiver explicitly agree regarding the bridge-building activity that, like in the case that follows, may include a blessing or a ritual.

What follows represents the situation faced by a Lutheran chaplain when asked to bless a deceased newborn child. The case study was originally presented as an example of how chaplains often seek to "reconcile" their theological convictions with care receivers' different spirituality in sound ministry practice. Study of the case revealed that the situation may also be viewed as a reframing of the chaplain's initial assumptions, facilitated by his disposition to provide compassionate care.

A Lutheran Chaplain Cares for a Spiritual-but-Not-Religious Woman

Alone in the room, sitting up in bed, was an Asian woman in her late 30s.

Chaplain: "Hello, I'm Jack, one of the hospital chaplains."

Patient: "Hi Jack. I'm Jane."

Chaplain: "I'm so sorry for your loss. I'm here to help you through this in any way I can."

Patient: (tearing up and weeping mildly) "Thanks, I appreciate that."

Chaplain: "The nurse told me you want a blessing for your baby."

Patient: (quietly) "Yes, I do."

Chaplain: "It's my privilege to help you with that. I want to accompany you as best I can."

Patient: (quietly) "Thanks."

Chaplain: "Can you share with me what it means to you to have your baby blessed? I mean, what do you wish for your child as I bless him?"

Patient: (a little more loudly) "It's about the gesture."

Chaplain: "Does the gesture come from any particular tradition?"

Patient: "No. I'm less religious than spiritual."

Chaplain: [following a brief exploration of this statement] "I understand now. That's helpful. Thank you."

Their conversation turned toward her general situation, until Jack departed the room while a nurse tended to Jane.

Jack faced an interesting situation. Jane did not even remotely refer to baptismal language or baptism. Could he, in good conscience, perform what she *wasn't* asking for? Part of this question came from the fact that he did not have "fetal demise blessing language" at his quick reference and use. The other issue was whether Jack fully understood what she meant by both "gesture" and "spiritual." Did he have enough information to feel confident that he could provide something to meet her need? It was not a question of whether or not he would do this for her, especially since he had already begun a pastoral relationship with her. Jack cherished the opportunity to provide compassionate care in the face of Jane's pain.

It is unnecessary for Lutherans to baptize deceased babies, but the common practice of doing so out of compassion for parents and respect for sacramental mystery had become Jack's reflexive response to fetal demise. What Jack knew and had previously experienced was, specifically, baptism. Jane's request for a non-specific spiritual "gesture" expanded this knowledge and experience as he discerned how to gladly and *in good conscience* provide something outside of his theological views and ecclesial practice. Having internally negotiated these doctrinal and spiritual hurdles, he felt ready to offer Jane compassionate and meaningful care.

A short time later, Jane's baby boy was returned to her. She, two of her friends, another chaplain, and Jack shared a meaningful and moving blessed ritual that included prayer for the boy, Jane, her absent husband (who was traveling and would join her soon), family, and friends. Jack had "reconciled" his doctrinal views, common practice, and Jane's spirituality, and he was grateful.

Caregivers' Code Switching

Strategies of mutually and explicitly minimizing difference and collaborative accommodation are deliberately co-created and enacted jointly by caregivers and care receivers. Code switching in interfaith spiritual care, in contrast, is a strategy used solely by caregivers at their own initiative; it is not normally discussed with care receivers as a chosen therapeutic communication technique or overarching approach. This strategy was illustrated in the first chapter of this book in the case of Chaplain Sally Fritsche: An atheist prays Christian prayers with, and for, relatives of a dying man. The chaplain's acknowledgement of their tradition plays a communicative and interpretive function. The case illustration that follows is between that of a Muslim man and a Christian chaplain in a maximum-security prison.[13]

An Evangelical Prison Chaplain Cares for a Muslim Man

Mr. Gates, who is serving a sixty-year sentence for drug trafficking, has just received a call from a family member that his son, DJ, was shot and killed during a drug deal gone wrong. It seems that his son has fallen victim to the same criminal lifestyle as his father. So, this father is in his cell overwhelmed with sadness and despair for having failed his son as well as himself. His other enormous challenge is trying to heal the relationship with his daughter, Mia, who has a lot of anger toward him, primarily because of his poor example as a father to her deceased brother.

Because the prison is on temporary lockdown, Mr. Gates is in his cell, and he appears depressed. His cell is moderately in order, but he's pacing it from front to back. His copy of the Holy Qur'an is open on his bed, his prayer rug is on the floor, and his eyes are slightly red. Chaplain Davis approaches him with caution, looking for the opportune moment to offer care and to discern his role in collaborating with him pastorally.

> Chaplain: Good afternoon, Mr. Gates. I received a call about the tragic news you received. My deepest condolences to you.
>
> Mr. Gates: Yeah, I f***** up, chap.
>
> Chaplain: You have your Qur'an open and your prayer rug on the floor. Did I interrupt you?
>
> Mr. Gates: Nah, you good, chap. Just messed up how they did my son like that. Ten times?
>
> Chaplain: Oh Lord, that's tragic. I'm sorry to hear that.

---

13. Rev. Damien W.D. Davis presented this case study during a DMin course, M609: Culturally Attentive Pastoral Leadership—Interfaith Pastoral Care & Counseling, at McCormick Theological Seminary in October 2021. See also Davis, "Prison Life."

Mr. Gates: It's cool. Allah has forgiven them. It's just going to take me time. What's f***** up, chap—all he had to do was listen to me on how to sell drugs and he'd be good. Now my daughter blames me for what happened.

Chaplain: Selling drugs never has had a good ending, but I don't think you need to focus on what you could have taught him. Maybe there's something you need to give more attention to?

Mr. Gates: What's that?

Chaplain: Your daughter. Right now, your daughter is angry that her brother is gone, and she could be angry with you for a different reason.

Mr. Gates: What would that be?

Chaplain: Perhaps your daughter misses her dad. Maybe the best thing you could do right now to please Allah is to try to heal the relationship with her.

Mr. Gates: I'll try, but we never got along really.

Chaplain: Somewhere I read in the Hadiths, "When the believer commits a sin, a black spot appears on his heart. If he repents and gives up that sin and seeks forgiveness, his heart will be polished. But if sin increases, the black spot increases."[14] So, what am I saying? Mr. Gates, perhaps it's best to start forgiving yourself for your absence, and work toward healing the relationship with your daughter.

Mr. Gates: Yeah, you right. That's a good idea.

Chaplain: [after further conversation] Is there anything I can do for you?

Mr. Gates: Nah, I think I'm good. But I appreciate you coming by to talk with me.

Chaplain: Sounds good, just keep me posted if you need anything.

Chaplain Davis reflected that his spiritual care approach deliberately included helping Mr. Gates to access and integrate spiritual resources from his religious-spiritual tradition in the face of critical circumstances. He also engaged the care receiver with an eye to moving forward toward healing the relationship with his daughter. The chaplain's reference to Islamic resources strengthened the relationship in terms of mutual trust and respect.

---

14. Vol. 5, Book 37, Hadith 4244. This is a reference to the collection of traditional sayings of the Prophet Muhammad, which, along with accounts of his daily practice (the Sunna) and the Qur'an, is the major source of guidance for Muslims.

Additionally, this encounter rekindled Davis's vision to gather focus groups of incarcerated men who desire a better relationship with their children.

The Question of Integrity in Code-Switching Strategies

By definition, code switching in spiritual care involves adopting and adapting someone else's language and frame of reference as a therapeutic communication approach. So the question can be raised of whether this is a form of, justifiably or not, misleading or deceiving the care receivers. Buddhist chaplain Monica Sanford helpfully addresses this question of authenticity often encountered regarding requests for a ritual, a blessing, or a prayer. How can we pray authentically to deities we don't believe in? She responds by explicating the notion of *as-if space*[15] with her reflection on the time that the wife of a man in ICU asked her to take his hand and say a prayer:

> The words, "Our Father, who art in heaven, hollowed be your name," came from a place of authenticity deep inside me. In that moment, if anything I said could be of comfort to him and his family, I would say it. And if God existed in the way Christians believe he does, I knew he would understand. I don't know if God heard me, but I know my professor did. He stilled and rested for the remainder of the Lord's prayer and for several minutes thereafter. His wife and mother thanked me. I left with a heavy heart, but knowing that if I were called upon to pray with Christians or Jews or Hindus, I would do so authentically . . . When I pray for someone, "May you have peace in Jesus Christ," I truly hope they find that peace exactly according to their beliefs. This is not a lie and it is not wrong speech. I doubt that the historical man called Jesus Christ was the Son of God, but I nevertheless hope for the care seeker's sake, that He is listening and granting lasting peace.[16]

Chaplains Sanford, Fritsche, and Davis have all demonstrated ways to aptly employ code switching as an interfaith caregiving strategy. In doing so, each was inspired and supported by adequate clinical training and, especially, by the normative framework of the wisdom traditions—Buddhist,

---

15. "As-if space" here means the momentary setting aside, "bracketing," or, better yet, holding one's belief system side-by-side with that of the caregiver's, while assuming the plausible nature of the latter. As in the following interfaith caregiving situation, a caregiver with a non-theocentric worldview may communicate with a believing care seeker in her or his terms, "as if" God really existed.

16. Sanford, "Secret Atheist," 219–20.

Unitarian Universalist, and Christian, respectively—that they consistently represent.

So far in this chapter we have reviewed strategies and approaches especially, although not exclusively, designed for interfaith care situations. At this point, a reminder by pastoral theologian Martin Walton is welcome: "In the contemporary fluidity of religious and secular worldviews, all pastoral, chaplaincy, and spiritual care should be considered interreligious, intercultural and intercontextual [intersectional] until proven otherwise."[17] The next section presents a number of ways of addressing such diversity and difference under the overarching category of cultivating spiritual reflection.

CULTIVATING SPIRITUAL REFLECTION

All spiritual care strategies and approaches offer opportunities while also presenting potential risks; and that is especially the case in interfaith situations. Normally, some combination of methods can be chosen in light of careful clinical discernment. This section discusses a caregiving approach focused on the ways we can "identify, access, engage, and evaluate spiritual thoughts, experiences, and resources at play in caregiving conversations," including within interfaith care.[18] The following paragraphs describe seven categories of therapeutic communication forms, often called *interventions* or *techniques*. They come from the fields of counseling and psychotherapy and are especially applicable in interfaith situations in diverse institutional settings. Of course, in actual practice these communication forms are employed dynamically within the flow of psycho-spiritual caregiving processes.[19]

Probing

Caregivers pose questions in order to elicit information or encourage further discussion of a given topic. The desired content can be factual information as well as emotions and feelings experienced by care receivers. This

---

17. Walton, "Encountering Difference," 63.

18. Gabriel and Bidwell, "Leading and Facilitating," 93.

19. These descriptions stem from my counseling work. See also Clinebell, *Basic Types of Pastoral Care*, 65–92; Liefbroer, *Interfaith Spiritual Care*, 171–92; and Walton, "Encountering Difference."

form of communication should aim for an optimal blend of contemplative (or "reverent") and clinical (or "scientific," inquiring) curiosity.

Reflecting

Responsive listening normally leads to communication of empathy and understanding. Simultaneously, and often implicitly, this intervention seeks confirmation that mutual understanding is actually happening. Reflecting can be expressed through such actions as paraphrasing and "echoing" (repeating).

Evaluating

Sometimes caregivers need to express value judgements regarding the nature of caregivers' behaviors or feelings. Direct, negative evaluative interventions (e.g., via statements or questions) can serve the purpose of necessary confrontation (e.g., in the face of abusive behavior or self-harm). Indirect evaluative comments can encourage an alternative course of action. Positive evaluation (e.g., by agreeing, complimenting, and/or affirming) can serve as a supportive and empowering[20] technique.

Supporting

Caregivers often seek to reassure, reduce intense emotions and feelings, and deescalate tension and anxiety. They thus remind care receivers that there are internal and external resources available to them, especially in situations of serious crisis, loss, and trauma. The very caregiving relationship thus becomes a primary source of support.

---

20. Within this repertoire of therapeutic communication form, *empowering* care receivers can be included as a combination of evaluative, advising/assigning, and performing categories, or as a separate category. In any case, the purpose of empowering interventions is to enable care receivers to build a stronger sense of psycho-spiritual worth, strength, and agency, and to encourage appropriate action in the search for wellbeing justice for themselves and their communities.

Clarifying and Interpreting

There is often a fine line separating and connecting these two types of therapeutic communication. Strictly speaking, interpretation (e.g., unveiling subconscious motives and meanings) happens more readily in psychodynamically oriented counseling and psychotherapy. More often than not, reframing seekers' messages blurs the distinction between clarifying and interpreting techniques.

Performing

All kinds of spiritual care, without exception, can include a particularly directive approach and interventions under appropriate circumstances. Diverse activities, either by care seekers' request or by caregivers' initiative, may define the latter's engagement as guides of the therapeutic process. These can include opportune self-disclosure (e.g., sharing a personal experience, value, or opinion) and leading spiritual practices (e.g., prayers, blessings, or rituals).

Advising and Assigning

The repertoire of directive approaches and interventions also includes actions such as providing useful information and making recommendations during a session or a visit. They may also give assignments (e.g., performing certain exercises or reading from a sacred text) between sessions or visits.

The chart at the end of this chapter comes from my counseling practice and can be applied to other caregiving specialties as well. It shows the connection between four main situations that commonly make caregiving necessary—disorientation, conflict, crisis, and loss—and the seven categories of caregiving interventions or techniques described above.

Regarding the actual flow of a caregiving relationship in which such interventions may be employed, a fundamental pattern of wise discernment—recognizable across cultures—was described in chapter 3 as involving the movements of contemplation, engagement, form-giving, emergence, and release. It remains to address the question of overall professional competence to care well in interfaith situations. The competence profile of wise interfaith caregivers is the focus of the next, final chapter of this book.

	Disorientation	Conflict/Struggle	Crisis/Trauma	Loss/Death
Probing	What are you looking for? How can I be helpful?	Are there spiritual resources to help you face this dilemma?	What do you need to feel safe right now?	How does your spiritual tradition respond to suffering?
Reflecting	I hear you say that you feel stuck	So, sometimes you feel helpless and even hopeless	You're feeling overwhelmed and very anxious	As you said, some tragedies are very hard to face
Supporting	We are here because we believe we can process this.... You are working at it.	Your anger is going to help make a way forward for you	I am here with you. God is here with you	I will be available whenever you wish to call
Evaluating	You are understandably feeling bad and guilty because. . .	It's a good thing that you are working on this	Life seems to be very unfair sometimes	It's helpful to cry and lament at a time like this
Clarifying, Interpreting	I wonder if there's a deep fear you're not acknowledging	I feel there's a part of you that doesn't want to move forward...	I get the impression that you're blaming yourself for what happened	I wonder whether sometimes you feel your faith is too weak
Assigning, Advising	What would you like to do next? This is something that has helped a number of people	Think of those times when you could count on strength and support	I recommend that you consult a doctor in order to make sure that...	It will be helpful to reorder your daily routine during this journey of grief
Performing	You seem to have options. Let's write the pros and cons on a piece of paper	Let's pretend that I'm God. What will you tell me?	Offering water Breathing exercises	Special blessing Ritual of lament

Caregiving interventions for spiritual reflection.

6

Fostering Interfaith Competence
A Journey toward Proficiency

A CONSTANT ISSUE THUS far in this book (though mostly implicit besides the introductory observations included in chapter 1) has been that of competence. Simply put, "competence" in interfaith care refers to a number of "competencies" that caregivers must have in order to care effectively in different interfaith situations. These sets of interrelated competencies correlate with institutional and programmatic standards, and they constitute what can be called a desirable profile of *professional wisdom*.[1] This chapter presents a thorough discussion of the competency profile, including the question of the holistic formation of interfaith caregivers. Its content can be viewed in connection with ongoing discussions of evidence-based[2] and outcome-driven[3] caregiving practice.

---

1. Schipani and Bueckert, *Interfaith Spiritual Care*, 315–19.

2. In the case of healthcare chaplaincy, a fairly comprehensive overview of research is found in Fitchett et al., *Evidence-Based Healthcare Chaplaincy*. An area still needing systematic research has to do with the epistemological and methodological issues pertaining to the theological/philosophical-ethical norms that all spiritual caregivers necessarily work with, most often implicitly. That research must focus especially on the connection between those sources of normativity (e.g., about the nature of reality, human wholeness and the good life, "good" suffering and dying well, etc.) and the psychological and psychotherapeutic norms and criteria employed, which are often made explicit in caregivers' self-reflection and in case studies particularly.

A critical observation made in chapter 1 of this book warrants repetition: Many spiritual caregivers, and chaplains in particular, can use *psychological* analyses of spirituality and "spiritual issues" while avoiding, or being unable to also employ *theological* reflection, narrowly or broadly speaking (that is, including non-theistic philosophical frameworks). That reflection, when adequately integrated to the psychological analysis, helps inform not only the assessment of spirituality and spiritual issues but the actual caregiving practice, as well as the appraisal of the whole caregiving process. In other words, it is an indispensable competence in all forms of spiritual care, and in interfaith spiritual care particularly.

3. Valued healthcare outcomes are currently associated with reduced costs, improved

Concerns related to research-informed and evidence-based caregiving practice—and of recognizable, valued outcomes for that practice—are, of course, closely connected. Competent spiritual caregivers are trained according to evidence-based standards, including attentiveness to the effects ("outcomes") of their care. They seek to become effectively equipped and resourced to care well and to evaluate the fruits of their labor as objectively as possible; this is a matter of ethical and professional responsibility and accountability. At the same time, it is important to keep in mind that spiritual caregivers—counselors, pastoral ministers, psychotherapists, chaplains, and others—cannot predict or orchestrate the results of their care. In any case, they still must have clarity regarding their own goals and must reflect critically on their effectiveness in reaching those goals.

The first part of this chapter has a section on cultural competence as originally proposed and developed in the field of intercultural counseling and psychotherapy.[4] It also includes a contribution from the psychologies of religion and spirituality and their application in clinical practice. The second part of the chapter presents the latest version of my work on competence in interfaith spiritual care. It is followed by a detailed illustration of how an international, intercultural, and interreligious association has moved to embrace intercultural and interfaith proficiency.

PROFILES OF (INTER)CULTURAL COMPETENCE

For more than three decades, a number of practitioners and researchers in the larger field of intercultural care and counseling have proposed necessary sets of core competencies in terms of the wider category of *cultural competence*. This is the case, for example, with the well-known contributions of Derald Wing Sue, David Sue, and research partners concerning multicultural competence in counseling practice. They define cultural competence as:

---

quality of care, patient experience (often measured by patient satisfaction), and/or enhanced health outcomes (often measured by cure rates, reduced length of stay, or reduced use of healthcare resources). See Handzo et al., "Outcomes."

4. Readers should keep in mind a rule of thumb concerning the connection between *intercultural* and *interfaith* caregiving: All the clinical and other learnings stemming from reflective practice and research in the field of intercultural care and counseling also pertain to interfaith care and counseling. Systematic research and writings on the former came first, however.

a lifelong process in which one works to develop the ability to engage in actions or create conditions that maximize the optimal development of clients and client systems. Multicultural counseling competence is aspirational and consists of counselors acquiring awareness, knowledge, and skills needed to function effectively in a pluralistic democratic society (ability to communicate, interact, negotiate, and intervene on behalf of clients from diverse backgrounds), and on an organizational level, advocating effectively to develop new theories, practices, policies, and organizational structures that are more responsive to all groups . . . *cultural competence* can be seen as residing in three major domains: (a) attitudes/beliefs component . . . ; (b) knowledge component . . . ; and skills component . . . Cultural humility serves as the conduit in which awareness, knowledge, and skills are expressed.[5]

The latest version of their contribution includes fourteen competencies under the categories of *awareness*,[6] *knowledge*, and *skills*, as identified below. Described in this light, culturally competent caregivers are:

- Aware of and sensitive to their own cultural heritage, and value and respect differences.

- Aware of their own values and biases and how they might affect diverse clients.

- Comfortable with differences that exist between themselves and their clients in terms of race, gender, sexual orientation, and other social identity variables. Differences are not seen as deviant.

- Sensitive to circumstances (personal biases; stage of racial, gender, and sexual orientation identity; sociopolitical influences, etc.) that may dictate referral of clients to members of their own social identity group(s) or to different therapists in general.

- Aware of their own racist, sexist, heterosexist, or other detrimental attitudes, beliefs, or feelings.

- Knowledgeable and informed on a number of culturally diverse groups, especially groups with whom therapists work.

---

5. Sue et al., *Counseling the Culturally Diverse*, 33–35. For a systematic, empirical study of cultural competence, see Deardorff, *SAGE Handbook*; and Deardorff, *Manual*.

6. The references seem to somehow identify the broad categories of "awareness" and "attitudes/beliefs"; the latter, however, is a broader psychological construct that includes the former; therefore, it is the preferred label.

- Knowledgeable about the local sociopolitical system's operation with respect to its treatment of marginalized groups in society.
- Possessing specific knowledge and understanding of the generic characteristics of counseling and therapy.
- Knowledgeable about the institutional barriers that prevent some diverse clients from using mental health and spiritual care services.
- Able to generate a wide variety of verbal and nonverbal helping responses.
- Able to communicate (through sending and receiving both verbal and nonverbal messages) accurately and appropriately.
- Able to exercise institutional intervention skills on behalf of clients, when appropriate.
- Able to anticipate the impact of their helping styles and their limitations with culturally diverse clients.
- Able to apply helping roles characterized by an active systemic focus, which leads to environmental interventions. They are not restricted by the conventional counselor/therapist mode of operation.[7]

Other researchers and clinicians have integrated similar profile proposals in terms of the caregivers' attitudes and awareness of their own values and biases, understanding of the clients' worldview, and developing culturally appropriate intervention strategies and techniques. Of particular interest to those involved in interfaith spiritual care are the contributions of Cassandra Vieten and Shelley Scammell.[8] Grounded in clinical research and practice, they helpfully describe, explain, and illustrate sixteen competencies within the categories of attitudes, knowledge, and skills:

- Demonstrating empathy, respect, and appreciation
- Appreciating religious and spiritual diversity
- Being aware of one's own beliefs and values
- Exploring diverse beliefs and practices

---

7. Sue et al., *Counseling the Culturally Diverse*, 34.

8. Vieten and Scammell, *Spiritual and Religious Competencies*. See also the reference to an eight-module online training program in Pearce et al., "Novel Training Program." The program focuses on sixteen competencies in terms of attitudes, knowledge, and skill necessary to care well in the face of religious and spiritual diversity.

- Knowing the difference between spirituality and psychopathology
- Understanding spirituality and religion as different but overlapping
- Recognizing lifespan development
- Learning about clients' spiritual and religious resources
- Recognizing harmful involvement
- Being aware of legal and ethical issues
- Working with spiritual and religious diversity
- Taking a religious and spiritual history
- Helping clients access their religious and spiritual resources
- Identifying spiritual and religious problems
- Staying up-to-date
- Acknowledging one's limits

The authors also include training guidelines, with indicators of growth, toward increasing competency for those involved in education and supervision. They can inform goals or expected outcomes in curriculum design and education, supervision, and continuing education in order to assess progress in cultivating those special competencies.[9]

During the last several years, my work on competence in interfaith spiritual care has taken into consideration contributions like those summarized above. That has been the case because interreligious or interfaith spiritual care can be understood as necessitating a special form of intercultural competence. At the same time, I have concluded that a more comprehensive frame of reference is necessary to better address the complexity, challenges, and promising potential of interfaith spiritual care. To that proposal we now turn our attention.

9. Vieten and Scammell, *Spiritual and Religious Competencies*, 181–87. For example, regarding the first competency—demonstrating empathy, respect, and appreciation for clients from diverse spiritual, religious, or secular backgrounds and affiliations—caregivers can demonstrate empathy, respect, and appreciation toward spiritual and religious material presented by their clients; they can define "empathy," "respect," and "appreciation" with regard to spiritual and religious beliefs and practices; they are willing to address and explore spiritual and religious issues presented by their clients and not avoid them; they can describe three methods for increasing empathy, respect, and appreciation with regard to their clients' spiritual and religious beliefs and practices; they can identify when their empathy, respect, or appreciation of religious and spiritual issues has been challenged and seek consultation or supervision when needed.

COMPETENCIES FOR WISE INTERFAITH SPIRITUAL CARE

The following paragraphs present a picture of excellence or *professional wisdom* based on both clinical practice and empirical research as well as broad consultation among colleagues. Wisdom in interfaith care involves not only what we know but also who we are and what we do. In other words, professional wisdom for excellent interfaith care may be viewed as the integration of three interconnected domains—*being, knowing,* and *doing*—as represented in the diagram below. This is the case concerning both the clinical (i.e., attitudes, knowledge, and skills that define expertise) as well as "ministerial" (i.e., vocational identity, philosophy of care, and consistent practice) dimensions connoted by "professional."

We can draw a portrait by focusing on a number of core competencies within each of these domains. The resulting profile of wise spiritual care consists of three sets of core competencies that can be identified in the course of spiritual care practice in teaching and supervision, in specialized research, and in extensive consultations and collaboration.

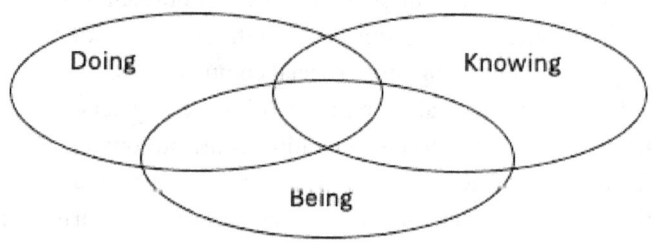

Three domains of core competencies.

INTERRELATED DOMAINS OF CORE COMPETENCIES

Competencies are dispositions and capacities necessary to care well in interfaith situations. Core competencies correlate with professional standards; those standards are normally articulated by governmental health-related departments and agencies as well as diverse professional organizations,[10] in-

---

10. In North America, the Association for Clinical Pastoral Education, the Association of Professional Chaplains, the Spiritual Care Association, the Canadian Association for Spiritual Care, and others.

cluding faith-based associations,[11] with their sets of normative professional standards of certification and practice for their members.

Standards embody key values and vocational commitments; they also prescribe certain legally binding professional and ethical requirements for effective caregiving. In summary, competencies are personal and professional qualities or assets with which caregivers meet the standards of practice in a wide variety of caregiving settings. Before proceeding with a characterization of core competencies, it is useful to keep in mind some normative guidelines that support the view of necessary competencies for wise spiritual care.

NORMATIVE GUIDELINES

The following normative guidelines serve as a rationale for the way we identify, seek to embody, discuss, teach, and assess core competencies in spiritual care that include but go beyond cultural competencies strictly speaking. Focusing on core competencies is not only a matter of *how* (i.e., functionality, how they "work" in actual caregiving practice) and *for what* (purpose, outcomes envisioned), but also a question of *why* (foundation, their reason for being). A threefold response to the *why* question follows.

First, core competencies are not only desirable *clinical-professional* features of excellence in spiritual care, but also indicators of a *personal, interpersonal, and institutional ethic*. Spiritual care is inherently partial in favor of wellness, quality of life, and meaningful suffering, healing, and dying. It is also partial toward compassion, peace, and justice, among other fundamental values. Spiritual care rightly viewed is also partial against meaningless and unnecessary suffering and dying, hopelessness, neglect, discrimination, and injustice. To be consistent with that realization calls for grounding core competencies explicitly in an *ethic of care and justice*. Therefore, becoming holistically competent is a moral imperative first and foremost. In fact, the absence of explicit ethical grounding and vocational commitment fosters a view of competence and competencies as merely a question of appropriate technique.

Second, *spiritual* care focuses primarily, although by no means exclusively, on *spirituality* and *spiritual experience*. For that reason, it is possible to work with an inclusive understanding of the *human spirit* that is not

11. The National Association of Catholic Chaplains, the National Association of Jewish Chaplains, and others.

collapsed into either our psychological views of "mind" or our theologically specific conceptualizations of "spirit." Ironically, in spite of so much discussion about replacing "pastoral" with "spiritual," a systematic reflection on the human spirit is hard to find in spiritual care literature! Chapter 2 of this book proposes one way to conceptualize *human spirit* inclusively (that is, with language not primarily reflective of a given religious tradition or theological orientation) that can be viewed functionally in terms of interrelated dimensions—*vision*, *virtue*, and *vocation*—within a social web and system.

The practice of spiritual care always includes the possibility of visualizing how the relationship of caregiver to care receiver might contribute to the latter's ongoing process of human emergence—that is, personal growth understood as lifelong "humanization," or becoming "more human," viewed contextually in the care receivers' terms. It follows that the desired outcomes of a counseling session or a spiritual caregiver's hospital visit, for instance, will include not only objectives such as neutralizing anxiety and evoking hope, but also supporting and resourcing the larger process of formation and transformation of the care receiver's *person as embodied psychosocial and spiritual self*. And that must be the case whether the care receiver faces recovery, or faces sickness and an uncertain diagnosis or treatment, or even death.

Third, core competencies must reflect the inherent normativity of spiritual care and the need to focus on spirituality and the human spirit. Accordingly, we can then articulate guidelines that call for *good*, *true*, and *right* qualities that define wise or competent spiritual care. By using the Greek prefix *ortho*, we might say that competencies must be identified in terms of: (a) *orthopathy* or *orthokardia* ("good heart": attitudes toward self and others, character strengths, etc., that make being genuinely present to care receivers and others possible); (b) a kind of *orthodoxy* (truthful beliefs and knowledge, duly contextualized, that foster understanding); and (c) *orthopraxis* (right action for effective strategy, performance, and assessment of spiritual care as an art of companioning). This is precisely the reason for adopting the categories of *being*, *knowing*, and *doing* in our work and reflection on core competencies in spiritual care.[12]

---

12. Schipani, *Multifaith Views*, 167–75.

A PROFILE OF CORE COMPETENCIES FOR WISE SPIRITUAL CARE

The categories of *being, knowing,* and *doing* help us to present a more complete view of holistic formation and professional wisdom than the one implied in the categories of *attitudes, knowledge,* and *skills* as presented before. That is especially the case regarding the being dimension, because in it we can include competencies definable in terms of virtues (that is, values embodied in the moral character of the caregiver) and faith development broadly viewed, which are not usually explicitly considered in current discussions and writings in the field. The following profile, which includes competencies also identified as such by others, is comprehensive but certainly not assumed to be complete, let alone final; it is meant as an ongoing collaborative work of reflection.[13]

Knowing Competencies (Understanding)

In order to grow in pastoral wisdom, interfaith spiritual caregivers participate in what we might call four "circles of learning": (1) the actual experience of caring and being cared for by others (learning by feeling); (2) observation and reflection on care provided by others (learning by seeing and hearing); (3) systematic analysis of those practices of care (learning by thinking); and (4) active experimentation with new ways of caring well for others (learning by doing). The more intentionally and consistently we participate in these circles, the more likely that our knowledge about interfaith care will increase. Supervision, seminars, and consultation groups can be fertile settings for developing knowledge and understanding related to spiritual care in interfaith situations. A sample of indicators of professional wisdom directly connected with this domain (*knowing*) include:

- A philosophy of spiritual care, including a view of human wholeness, truth, the good life, and excellence in professional work (as seen especially in an ethic of care), grounded in one's faith tradition and informed by other wisdom traditions.

---

13. See Cadge and Rambo, *Chaplaincy and Spiritual Care,* 61–189. The nineteen competencies they discuss and illustrate are also necessary for caregiving work in other forms of spiritual care such as counseling and psychotherapy, especially in interfaith situations.

- Theoretical integration of spirituality, behavioral and social science, and philosophical and theological perspectives that include a four-dimensional view of reality and knowing.
- Understanding of the complexities, dynamics, and richness of interfaith situations, with recognition of human and spiritual commonalities and due consideration to gender, culture, religious, family, and social and political contexts.
- Philosophical and theological assessment that includes revisiting the validity of certain absolute, normative doctrinal claims; selective reappropriation of theological and religious convictions; and rediscovery of the simplicity and beauty of core spiritual clues for interfaith care.
- Linguistic-conceptual and "multilingual" competency (knowing a variety of psychological, theological, and spiritual languages) born out of theological and human science perspectives and resources.
- Clinical ways of knowing, such as interpretive frameworks (psychodynamic, systemic, cognitive-behavioral, etc.) that enhance understanding, communication, and professional/ministerial practice of spiritual care.
- Research literacy in order to read, understand, and apply basic research to one's caregiving practice.

Such comprehensive ways of *knowing* must always be closely related to the *being* and *doing* dimensions of professional wisdom, as briefly considered below.

Being Competencies (Presence)

Professional wisdom is also a matter of "being" as well as "being with" that defines *presence*. Caregiving in interfaith situations involves special sensitivity and self-awareness regarding what one feels and experiences in the relationship. It also involves the sense that one represents not only a religious tradition and community but also, somehow, healing grace. We deem such embodiment essential to remind care receivers that a caring presence is available. Therefore, a sense of personal and professional/ministerial identity and authority are an essential component of being and presence. It is indispensable to engage the care receiver in a relationship characterized first of all by respectfully attending and listening. Such a relationship allows the spiritual caregiver to be a witness, not there to tell care receivers how to cope with or fix their situation, but rather to "admire"—to behold with love and hope the mystery that is the stranger. Among the traits related to the *being* dimension of professional wisdom, I find the following to be essential:

- Self-awareness and other indicators of emotional and social intelligence, including acknowledgment of strengths and limitations; movement beyond preoccupation with one's "ministerial-therapeutic" self, while maintaining clarity regarding identity as spiritual caregiver; recognition of ways in which one's professional/ministerial identity influences the interfaith encounter; and quietude.

- Moral character that integrates a plurality of attitudes and virtues, such as a capacity for wonder and respect in the face of the stranger; sensitivity and receptivity; courage to risk and to be surprised; freedom to be vulnerable and open to learning and growth; a disposition to recognize, accept, and honor those deemed to be different; hospitality grounded in compassion, humility, patience, and generosity; passion to care and creative energy to transform the inherent violence of separation, prejudice, and alienation into a way of being with (empathy) and for (sympathy) the other as neighbor and partner in care and healing; and living out "sacred teachings" such as love, respect, courage, humility, truth, honesty, and wisdom.[14]

- Spirituality defined partly in terms of a mature and "conjunctive faith" that informs clinical style[15] and denotes a desirable level of faith development. This includes an ability to embrace ambiguity and paradox; a sense of truth that is multiform and complex; post-critical receptivity ("second naiveté") and readiness to participate in the reality expressed in symbols, myths, and rituals of one's own tradition; genuine and disciplined openness to the truths of communities and traditions other than one's own (not to be equated with relativism); and movement from the prevalence of certainty to the centrality of trust.

- A sense of personal and spiritual wellbeing, integrity, and growth. (While being aware of their own woundedness, wise spiritual

---

14. The notion of sacred teaching comes from Aboriginal spiritual caregiving colleagues. See McKellar and Armitte, "Journey toward Creator."

15. Fowler, *Stages of Faith*, 184–98; and Fowler, *Faith Development*, 71–74, 92–98.

caregivers normally experience holistic wellness of body, soul, and spirit and an existentially fruitful and fulfilling life journey.)

- A connection or a sense of association and co-participation with a transcendent Source of wisdom and grace; dedication to one's own awakening; and appropriate devotion to one's mentors or gurus.

Doing Competencies (Companioning)

Accompaniment and *guidance* are words that name well what we actually do in spiritual care. Guidance is a form of leading that includes setting appropriate boundaries of time, space, and contact, while remaining fully aware of what is going on in the caregiving process. Guidance may include gently probing questions, encouragement and support, instructing, confronting, and mediating. However, except in emergency or crisis situations, spiritual caregivers will not be directive and try to resolve the problems and struggles faced by care receivers. Rather, especially in interfaith situations, wise caregivers will help patients and others use the specific spiritual resources that have been part of their lives or that may now be available for them.

In short, accompaniment and guidance will optimally be a practice of wisdom—knowing how to relate and act in order to care well in interfaith situations. There is actually an interesting etymological connection between *wisdom* and *guidance*. In English, the words *wisdom* and *wise* derive from the Indo-European root *weid-*, which means "to see" or "to know." They are related to the Greek *eidos* ("idea," "form," "seeing"), to the Latin *videre* ("to see"), and to the modern German *wissen* ("to know"). The word *guide* comes from an ancient Romanic word *widare*, which means "to know." In short, the words *wise, wisdom, wit,* and *guide* all share the same origin. Therefore, among other competencies and skills, effective caregivers will be able to:

- Relate to care seekers, their relatives, and one's colleagues in ways that engage their spirituality and facilitate spiritual assessment, including the skill to articulate desired, evidence-based outcomes of spiritual care.

- Empower care receivers by reflecting together on the power imbalance inherent in the therapeutic relationship.

- Internally monitor ongoing caregiving practice so as to remain care receiver-centered, avoid cultural and spiritual invasion or intrusiveness, and be open to receiving manifold gifts from care receivers even while caring well for them.
- Actively listen and discern the appropriateness and timeliness of specific caregiving gestures, use of language, and action. Fittingly provide opportune responses in a variety of caregiving modes (e.g., probing, supporting, encouraging, comforting, guiding, confronting, mediating, reconciling, evoking, advocating, praying, blessing, anointing, and others).
- Reflect pastorally-theologically on ministerial and professional practice on an ongoing basis and continually develop a practical theology of interfaith care, including assessment, consultation, and collaboration.
- Actively emulate or partner with a transcendent Source of Wisdom and Grace or, for theist caregivers, the Spirit of God while anticipating and participating in caregiving ministry (e.g., by privately praying for oneself and for care seekers, engaging in contemplation and meditation, and other spiritual disciplines).
- Maintain patterned practices of self-care with adequate attention to physical, emotional, and relational needs and to spiritual nourishment; consistently participate in a community that offers psychosocial and spiritual nurture, support, and accountability.

Finally, we must also keep in mind two additional key considerations related to timing and level of proficiency. First, concerning timing, some competencies relate especially, although not exclusively, to what is expected to happen either before, during, or after spiritual caregiving practice. Second, in order to teach, practice, and assess core competencies, it is possible and, indeed, necessary to identify increasing levels of proficiency and guideposts to mark professional growth.

HOLISTIC FORMATION OF INTERFAITH CAREGIVERS

It has become more and more apparent that the education of interfaith spiritual caregivers in professional wisdom requires that theological education and clinical and ministerial formation be holistic and comprehensive. Such formation must include three equally important and interrelated aspects:

academic-interdisciplinary, personal-spiritual, and clinical-professional. Further, such education must include specific pedagogies of interpretation and contextualization, formation, and performance.

The *academic-interdisciplinary* formation of interfaith caregivers is indispensable because, among other things, it includes learning about one's own (religious or nonreligious) faith tradition or heritage, and as much as possible about other traditions. Philosophies, theoretical frameworks, and other resources stemming from the human sciences are also indispensable. Academic-interdisciplinary formation further includes learning about the social, cultural, and institutional contexts of caregiving work. Therefore, this dimension of clinical education and formation must focus primarily, although by no means exclusively, on learning and developing competencies of *knowing* for wise caregiving as highlighted above.

Personal-spiritual formation focuses on the identity and integrity of interfaith spiritual caregivers, especially but not exclusively as representatives of a given tradition. Personal-spiritual formation primarily involves attending to oneself as a human and spiritual being and nurturing one's moral character and vocation. Hence, this dimension of education and ministerial formation is concerned primarily with fostering and nurturing the competencies of *being* for wise ministry practice. Indeed, those competencies will directly inform the content of specific curricular learning goals toward personal-spiritual formation.

The *clinical-professional* formation of wise spiritual caregivers centers on the development of clinical and other habits, skills, methods, and approaches necessary for caring effectively and faithfully. Therefore, the third aspect of theological education and ministerial formation of interfaith spiritual caregivers must focus primarily on the development and practice of competencies of performance—the *doing* dimension of the profile—as the main curricular goal. The following diagram represents the holistic formation of interfaith spiritual caregivers with three interrelated dimensions.

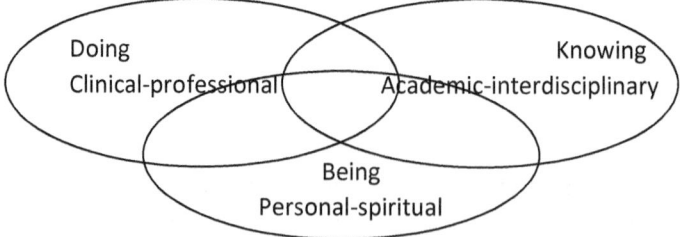

Holistic formation of interfaith spiritual caregivers.

COMPLEMENTARY PEDAGOGIES

It is clear that these three resulting sets of goals of theological education and ministerial or professional formation must be duly integrated and approached through appropriate, mutually complementary pedagogies. Reflection on pedagogies for educating clergy[16] can be helpfully applied broadly, for instance in Clinical Pastoral Education programs, to the formation of wise spiritual caregivers as described below.

Pedagogies of interpretation focus the attention of caregivers, as interpreters, on their interaction with their own tradition and with other sources of knowledge, particularly their relationship with care seekers. These pedagogies cultivate the abilities to adequately "read" and analyze human situations, and to think and reflect critically and creatively. They are aimed at expanding and deepening *understanding* through interpretive practice. *Pedagogies of contextualization* are closely related, as they seek to develop a spiritual caregiver's consciousness of context, the ability to participate constructively in the encounter of diverse contexts, and the ability to engage in the transformation of contexts. From the students' perspective, academic formation that is primarily fostered by pedagogies of interpretation and contextualization—including supervision in clinical education and advanced training in spiritual care—constitutes the curricular realm of "theory," theoretical learning, and knowing. It should be noted that I am intentionally using three categories—theory, experience, and practice—as fittingly holding the dimensions of theoretical, experiential, and practical wisdom normally described in educational theory as complementary ways of learning and knowing.

Pedagogies of formation aim at fostering personal integrity and vocational-professional identity. Specific strategies that contribute to the formation of ministering caregivers, especially those representing certain religious traditions, may include: awakening students to a sense of transcendence and/or the presence of the Divine; practicing holiness, i.e., nurturing dispositions and habits that embody philosophical-ethical (and/or religious) commitments integral to the identity of ministering persons; and practicing spiritual leadership in which one's very *presence* communicates Grace and Wisdom. Therefore, students' personal-spiritual formation will be supported primarily with pedagogies of formation within the curricular realm of "experience"—experiential learning and knowing.

---

16. See Foster et al., *Educating Clergy,* 67–186.

Finally, *pedagogies of performance* focus on the interaction of academic and religious expectations for effective leadership in ministerial practice. They seek to prepare caregivers to be proficient in meeting a wide variety of expectations for excellence in interfaith care within multifaith settings. In sum, they are learning strategies aimed at equipping caregivers for the ministerial art of *companioning*. Vocational-professional formation sustained with pedagogies of performance will therefore pertain to the curricular realm of "practice"—practical learning and knowing.

Together with attention to intercultural and interfaith competence development among practitioners and theoreticians, it is necessary to focus on the need for change, indeed transformation, among formation settings (universities, theological seminaries, healthcare centers, and others), spiritual care associations and organizations, and especially accrediting and licensing bodies. Increasing inclusiveness and broadening of perspectives and horizons will take place as a function of intentional disempowerment regarding dominant worldviews, languages, narratives, and structures. The following section is offered as a case study of an ongoing journey to intercultural and interfaith proficiency embarked upon by an international association.

COLLEGIAL ASSOCIATIONS AS NURTURING SETTINGS: THE CASE OF THE SIPCC

The first part of this section highlights some key developments in the life of the Society for Intercultural Pastoral Care and Counseling from the perspective of an active member during the last twenty years.[17] The second part briefly discusses a key transition in the unfolding story of the Society—namely, a movement from competence toward proficiency.[18]

---

17. I joined the SIPCC during my participation in its 2005 International Seminar in Düsseldorf, Germany, the theme of which was "Intercultural and Interfaith Communication." The program included a workshop—"Intercultural Reading of the Bible"—that I was invited to present. The content of the workshop stemmed from the results of an empirical research project in which I participated primarily from a practical theological perspective. See de Wit et al., *Through the Eyes of Another*.

18. More recently, the International Association for Spiritual Care was formed with the mission to enhance the capacities of scholars and practitioners worldwide in acquiring, disseminating, and applying knowledge of theory and practice of spiritual care with an emphasis on interdisciplinary, interreligious, and intercultural scholarly investigation. The Association offers continuing education opportunities, encourages networks for professional support and enrichment, and facilitates growth and interdisciplinary

Highlights of a Fruitful Journey

The SIPCC offers a welcoming space for collegial encounter, dialogue, and collaboration. Among associations with similar interests, two features stand out: first, the SIPCC has a continuous, yearly agenda that includes education programs in several countries in Europe, Africa, and Asia; and second, it has attracted participants with diverse training and specializations without imposing hierarchical categories. As a result, the Society functions as a multicultural laboratory that fosters intercultural and interreligious communication on multiple levels.

Over the years, SIPCC members have benefitted both personally and vocationally from active participation. A number of fruitful interactions in workshops and lectureships, especially connected to the Hamburg (Germany, 2006) and Bratislava (Slovakia, 2008) seminars, led to the publication of the first major text in English on interfaith spiritual care.[19] The following year, the first major manual on the subject in German was published.[20] The research agenda thus became more systematic regarding its *interreligious* or *interfaith*[21] focus on intercultural communication and caregiving processes.

By 2013 the efforts to foster interreligious communication became a priority, as reflected in the Mainz (Germany) international seminar. That conference convened under the umbrella title, "Islamic Spiritual Care: A 'Trialogue' Between Muslims, Jews, and Christians." The same year the SIPCC sponsored the publication of a book with contributions from representatives of seven different traditions.[22] In the meantime, the SIPCC

---

innovation engaging medicine, psychology, theology, nursing, and social work. (iasc.org) Despite differences in structure, organization, and agendas, the overarching goals of these two organizations, SIPCC and IASC, are compatible and, in some ways, complementary.

19. Schipani and Bueckert, *Interfaith Spiritual Care*. The book was published in collaboration with the SIPCC and was dedicated to Helmut Weiss as an "ecumenically minded and collaborative pioneer in the field of intercultural and interfaith spiritual care."

20. Weiß et al., *Handbuch Interreligiöse Seelsorge*. The SIPCC had published a major book on intercultural pastoral care a few years earlier: Federschmidt et al., *Handbuch Interkulturelle Seelsorge*.

21. While in Europe and Latin America the term "interreligious" is used, in the United States and Canada the tendency has been to use "interfaith" instead, as "faith" may include the category of non-religious belief system.

22. Schipani, *Multifaith Views*.

mission statement had been amended to include the term "interreligious," as had many titles and themes of subsequent international seminars.[23] By the twentieth-year celebration, a new publication was fittingly entitled, *Intercultural and Interreligious Pastoral Caregiving: The SIPCC 1995–2015: 20 Years of International Practice and Reflection*.[24] The latest contribution to the field is an even more comprehensive and inclusive text: *Care, Healing, and Human Well-Being within Interreligious Discourses.*[25]

Other significant developments during the last several years can also be documented, for example, regarding the complex realities and challenges of migration. The theme was explored as the main focus of consideration in the Strasbourg (France, 2010) and Gent (Belgium, 2016) conferences. During the latter, another major publication project was conceived. In addition to ten SIPCC members, guest contributors included both practitioners and scholars.[26] Issues related to conflict, violence, peace with justice and reconciliation, decolonization, and ecofeminism, among others, are addressed as well.

From Competence to Proficiency

One way to characterize the forward movement of the SIPCC story is to apply categories stemming from social science research on intercultural competence. The following observations are offered more as a hypothesis than an assessment.

From the beginning, the work of the SIPCC has sought to include adequate levels of intercultural competence within the three areas already discussed in this chapter: knowledge (cultural self-awareness, culture-specific knowledge, socio-linguistic awareness, grasp of global issues and trends, etc.); attitudes (respect and valuing other cultures and religions, openness, curiosity, tolerance of ambiguity, etc.); and skills (listening, observing, careful evaluation, viewing the world from others' perspectives, etc.). As already discussed, those sets of categories have been included within the larger categories of knowing, being, and doing, respectively. However, the question of identifiable steps in the movement toward intercultural and interfaith proficiency still needs to be addressed.

23. SIPCC, "Mission Statement."
24. Federschmidt and Louw, *Intercultural and Interreligious Pastoral Caregiving*.
25. Weiss et al., *Care, Healing, and Human Well-Being*.
26. Schipani et al., *Where are We?*

Fostering Interfaith Competence

Social scientists help us to define intercultural competence developmentally—that is, as a movement from "monocultural" mindsets to "cultural integration," with the capacity to facilitate appropriate and effective communication in intercultural interactions. A practical resource for our purpose is the model of "Intercultural Development Continuum," which supplies the overarching framework for assessment with the "Intercultural Development Inventory."[27] Research on intercultural competency and the resulting theory thus offers a framework to evaluate major developments in the trajectory of professional and academic associations such as the SIPCC.[28]

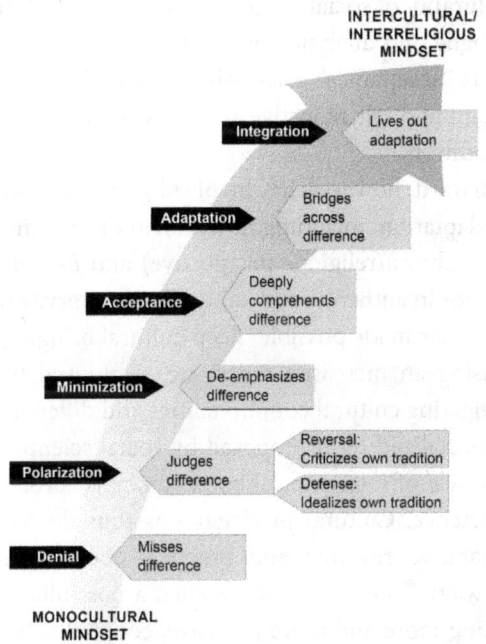

Developmental model of interreligious competence.

27. Intercultural Development Inventory, "About Us." Designed and validated by Milton J. Bennet and Mitchell R. Hammer, the inventory is the assessment tool for the Developmental Model of Intercultural Sensitivity (DMIS) created by Bennett. See Bennett, "Developmental Model." The DMIS describes a process of growth in how people experience and respond to cultural differences. For an important application and adaptation of the DMIS, see Morgan and Sandage, "Developmental Model."

28. The diagram is an adaptation of the one created by Mitchell R. Hammer, PhD, President of Intercultural Development Inventory. It should be noted that progression toward adaptation and integration is rarely a continuous, smooth, and one-directional movement.

According to this model and the current SIPCC's stated and public "self-understanding,"[29] the Society seeks to foster the highest level of intercultural and interreligious mindset. At the same time, it can be argued that both in actual practice as well as in terms of self-understanding, the SIPCC has experienced considerable progress in moving from "acceptance" toward "adaptation" and "integration."

During the earlier years, the Society's contributions significantly unveiled the distinct realities and dynamics of European and other social-cultural contexts of care and counseling, primarily with a Christian worldview and from a Christian perspective. Recognition, understanding, and appreciation of the plurality of social contexts were paramount. Intentional and systematic dialogue and analytic comparisons were, and continue to be, indispensable. Its "acceptance" orientation included, and continues to include, a significant and self-reflective and critical look at one's own culture and religious tradition.

Moving forward, however, has involved going beyond acceptance to what is called adaptation, including in the form of *cognitive frame-shifting* (changing one's cultural/religious perspective) and *behavior code-shifting* (changing behavior in authentic and culturally appropriate ways). "Adaptation" thus viewed has made possible "deep cultural bridging across diverse communities using an increased repertoire of cultural frameworks and practices in navigating cultural commonalities and differences."[30]

Another specialized term proposed by social scientists to characterize the higher levels of intercultural competency is "proficiency" beyond adequate competence. Cultural proficiency is thus described as making possible collaborative research and practical cooperation in mutually transformative ways. To become reality, such a possibility requires major effort at becoming more and more inclusive, coupled with a considerable measure of voluntary self-disempowerment. In the SIPCC's case, active participation of Muslim colleagues during recent years and being hosted by the Islamic Cultural Centre in Vienna in 2018 have been important factors in moving forward. This movement is analogous to the change from predominantly Christian chaplaincy as the reigning paradigm of spiritual care in medical centers and other healthcare institutions, to that of multifaith teams able to offer effective and satisfactory intercultural and interfaith spiritual care.

29. See SIPCC, "Mission Statement."
30. SIPCC, "Mission Statement."

Finally, it is worth noting that the unfolding SIPCC story demonstrates a commitment to continued progress toward becoming what is stated in the Society's declaration of self-understanding: an *open space* for personal and institutional encounters and relationships, and for development of hermeneutics of intercultural and interreligious care and counseling; *areas of learning in difference* (language and communication, culture, religion); a *learning experience* in intercultural and interreligious competence; and a *learning community* in spirituality and in pastoral care and counseling as a socially relevant practice for our times.[31]

CONCLUSION: THE WAY FORWARD

In the face of rapid social change, there is a felt need today for designing new programs aimed at the formation of competent professional spiritual caregivers working in late modern and increasingly secular and multifaith contexts. At the same time, it is another priority to care well for those people who represent particular religious traditions, including hybrid and "fluid" spirituality, and those who identify themselves as non-religious spiritual people. Indeed, there is an evolving twofold movement in that direction, particularly in Europe, Canada, and the United States. On the one hand, in addition to programs associated with the Christian faith, we now find others connected with different religious traditions, such as Judaism, Islam, Hinduism, and Buddhism. They can prepare caregivers primarily, although not exclusively, for *intra-faith* spiritual care.[32] In most instances, those programs also seek to equip students for *interfaith* work carried out from the perspective of their tradition. On the other hand, new initiatives are also emerging that focus primarily on interfaith care, especially in university settings and medical centers; they can also offer the option for students to further their training within their own faith tradition, including Humanism.

---

31. SIPCC, "Mission Statement."

32. Regarding Muslim caregivers addressing Muslim populations primarily, see Al-Karam, *Islamically Integrated Psychotherapy*; Ahmed and Amer, *Counseling Muslims*; Isgandarova, *Muslim Women*; and Rassool, *Islamic Counselling*. Regarding Jewish spiritual care, see Levitz and Twerski, *Rabbinic Counseling*; Friedman, *Jewish Pastoral Care*; and Friedman and Yehuda, *Art of Jewish Pastoral Counseling*. Concerning Hindu approaches, see Sutton et al., *Hindu Chaplaincy*; and Chander and Mosher, *Hindu Approaches*. For a thorough presentation of Buddhist chaplaincy see Sanford, *Kalyanamitra*.

In addition to curriculum development and the strengthening of clinical practice as such, another priority is to focus on the specific dynamics of intercultural and interfaith clinical supervision. This agenda includes the variables involved in the supervisory relationship itself, as well as the consideration of group dynamics that foster intercultural and interfaith competency. In sum, given the need for balancing and mutually enriching interfaith spiritual care with its manifold challenges and opportunities in the years ahead, it is expected that spiritual care as a discipline will be significantly enhanced as well. It is, therefore, an exciting time to be part of such a life-giving movement!

Bibliography

Ahmed, Sameera, and Mona M. Amer, eds. *Counseling Muslims: Handbook of Mental Health Issues and Interventions*. New York: Routledge, 2012.

Alberta, Tim. *The Kingdom, the Power, and the Glory: American Evangelicals in an Age of Extremism*. San Francisco: Harper, 2023.

Ali, Muhammad A., Omer Bajwa, Sondos Kholaki, and Jaye Starr. *Mantle of Mercy: Islamic Chaplaincy in North America*. West Conshohocken, PA: Templeton, 2022.

Al-Karam, Carrie York. *Islamically Integrated Psychotherapy: Uniting Faith and Professional Practice*. West Conshohocken, PA: Templeton, 2018.

American Psychiatric Association. *Diagnostic and Statistical Manual of Mental Disorders (DSM-5)*. 5th ed. Washington, DC: American Psychiatric, 2013.

Antoun, Richard T. *Understanding Fundamentalism: Christian, Islamic, and Jewish Movements*. 2nd ed. New York: Rowman & Littlefield, 2008.

Ariarajah, S. Wesley. *Not Without My Neighbor: Issues in Interfaith Relations*. Geneva, Switzerland: World Council of Churches, 1999.

Armstrong, Karen. *The Battle for God: A History of Fundamentalism*. New York: Knopf, 2000.

Aten, Jamie D., and Mark M. Leach. *Spirituality and the Therapeutic Process: A Comprehensive Resource from Intake to Termination*. Washington, DC: American Psychological Association, 2009.

Augsburger, David W. *Pastoral Counseling Across Cultures*. Philadelphia: Westminster, 1986.

Barnett, John. *Christian and Sikh: A Practical Theology of Multiple Religious Participation*. Durham, UK: Sacristy, 2021.

Bass, Dorothy C., et al. *Christian Practical Wisdom: What It Is, Why It Matters*. Grand Rapids: Eerdmans, 2016.

Bass, Dorothy C., and Craig Dykstra, eds. *For Life Abundant: Practical Theology, Theological Education, and Christian Ministry*. Grand Rapids, Eerdmans, 2008.

Benner, David G. *Soulful Spirituality: Becoming Fully Alive and Deeply Human*. Grand Rapids: Brazos, 2011.

Bennett, Milton J. "Developmental Model of Intercultural Sensitivity." In *The International Encyclopedia of Intercultural Communication*, edited by Kim Young Yun, 1–10. London: John Wiley and Sons, 2017.

Bergen, Doris L. *Between God and Hitler: Military Chaplains in Nazi Germany*. Cambridge: Cambridge University Press, 2023.

Bidwell, Duane R. *When One Religion Isn't Enough: The Lives of Spiritually Fluid People*. Boston: Beacon, 2018.

Bidwell, Duane R., and Daniel S. Schipani. "Interreligious Care in Totalitarian Contexts: Learnings from Vietnam and Cuba." In *The Art of Spiritual Care Across Religious Difference*, edited by Jill L. Snodgrass, 131–52. Minneapolis: Fortress, 2024.

Blumenthal, David R. "Soul Repair: A Jewish View." In *Exploring Moral Injury in Sacred Texts*, edited by Joseph McDonald, 33–46. London: Jessica Kingsley, 2017.

Bibliography

Boelhower, Gary J. *Choose Wisely: Practical Insights from Spiritual Traditions*. New York: Paulist, 2013.
Boff, Leonardo. *Trinity and Society*. Translated by Paul Burns. Maryknoll, NY: Orbis, 1988.
Borg, Marcus J. *The Heart of Christianity: Rediscovering a Life of Faith*. San Francisco: Harper, 2003.
———. *Jesus: A New Vision: Spirit, Culture, and the Life of Discipleship*. San Francisco: Harper, 1987.
———. *Meeting Jesus Again for the First Time: The Historical Jesus and the Heart of Contemporary Faith*. San Francisco: Harper, 1994.
Bourdieu, Pierre. *Outline of a Theory of Practice*. Translated by Richard Nice. Cambridge: Cambridge University Press, 1977.
Brest, Martin, dir. *Scent of a Woman*. 1992; Universal City, CA: Universal Pictures. DVD.
Brock, Rita Nakashima. Prologue to *The Bible and Moral Injury: Reading Scripture Alongside War's Unseen Wounds*, by Brad E. Kelle, xi–xii. Nashville: Abingdon, 2020.
Brock, Rita Nakashima, and Gabriella Lettini. *Soul Repair: Recovering from Moral Injury After War*. Boston: Beacon, 2012.
Brown, Warren S., ed. *Understanding Wisdom: Sources, Science, & Society*. West Conshohocken, PA: Templeton, 2000.
Brown, William P. *Wisdom's Wonder: Character, Creation, and Crisis in the Bible's Wisdom Literature*. Grand Rapids: Eerdmans, 2014.
Browning, Don S. *A Fundamental Practical Theology*. Philadelphia: Fortress, 1991.
———. *Religious Thought and the Modern Psychologies: A Critical Conversation in the Theology of Culture*. Philadelphia: Fortress, 1987.
Browning, Don S., and Terry D. Cooper. *Religious Thought and the Modern Psychologies*. 2nd ed. Minneapolis: Fortress, 2004.
Brueggemann, Walter. *Spirituality of the Psalms*. Minneapolis: Fortress, 2002.
———. *Theology of the Old Testament: Testimony, Dispute, Advocacy*. Minneapolis: Fortress, 1997.
Bueckert, Leah D., and Daniel S. Schipani, eds. *Spiritual Caregivers in the Hospital: Windows to Competent Practice*. 3rd ed. Kitchener, ON: Pandora, 2022.
———, eds. *You Welcomed Me: Interfaith Spiritual Care in the Hospital*. Kitchener: Pandora, 2010.
Cadge, Wendy, and Shelly Rambo, eds. *Chaplaincy and Spiritual Care in the Twenty-First Century: An Introduction*. Chapel Hill: University of North Carolina Press, 2022.
Cadge, Wendy, and Emily Sigalow. "Negotiating Religious Differences: The Strategies of Interfaith Chaplains in Healthcare." *Journal for the Scientific Study of Religion* 52.1 (2013), 146–58.
Callaway, Kutter, and William B. Whitney. *Theology for Psychology and Counseling: An Invitation to Holistic Christian Practice*. Grand Rapids: Baker Academic, 2022.
Canadian Association for Spiritual Care. "Competencies of CASC/ACSS Certified Professionals." 2019.
Caperon, John, Andrew Todd, and James Walters, eds. *A Christian Theology of Chaplaincy*. London: Jessica Kingsley, 2017.
Caplan, Gerald. *Principles of Preventive Psychiatry*. New York: Basic, 1964.
Capps, Donald. *Deadly Sins and Saving Virtues*. Philadelphia: Fortress, 1987.
———. *The Decades of Life: A Guide to Human Development*. Louisville, KY: Westminster John Knox, 2008.

BIBLIOGRAPHY

Ceresko, Anthony R. *Introduction to Old Testament Wisdom: A Spirituality for Liberation*. Maryknoll: Orbis, 1999.

Chander, Vineet, and Lucinda Mosher, eds. *Hindu Approaches to Spiritual Care*. London: Jessica Kingsley, 2019.

Chittister, Joan. *Welcome to the Wisdom of the World And Its Meaning for You: Universal Spiritual Insights Distilled from Five Religious Traditions*. Grand Rapids: Eerdmans, 2007.

Clements, Ronald E. *Wisdom in Theology*. Grand Rapids: Eerdmans, 1993.

Clinebell, Howard. *Basic Types of Pastoral Care and Counseling: Resources for the Ministry of Healing and Growth*. Updated and revised by Bridget Clare McKeever. Nashville: Abingdon, 2011.

Cobb, Mark. "Critical Response to the Use of Ritual Case Studies—A Chaplain's Perspective." In *Case Studies in Spiritual Care: Healthcare Chaplaincy Assessments, Interventions, and Outcomes*, edited by George Fitchett and Steve Nolan, 212–21. London: Jessica Kingsley, 2018.

Cooper-White, Pamela. *The Psychology of Christian Nationalism: Why People Are Drawn In and How to Talk Across the Divide*. Minneapolis: Fortress, 2022.

Crenshaw, James L. *Sipping from the Cup of Wisdom*. 2 vols. Macon, GA: Smith & Helwys, 2017.

Csikszentmihalyi, Mihaly, and Isabella Selega Csikszentmihalyi, eds. *A Life Worth Living: Contributions to Positive Psychology*. Oxford: Oxford University Press, 2006.

Davis, Damien W.D. "Prison Life and the Aftermath of Thug Living: Chaplaincy Training Approaches for the Long-Term Incarcerated." DMin thesis, McCormick Theological Seminary, 2023.

de Wit, Hans, Louis Jonker, Marleen Kool, and Daniel Schipani, eds. *Through the Eyes of Another: Intercultural Reading of the Bible*. Elkhart: Institute of Mennonite Studies, 2004.

Deardorff, Darla K. *Manual for Developing Intercultural Competencies: Story Circles*. New York: Routledge, 2020.

———. *The SAGE Handbook of Intercultural Competence*. Thousand Oaks, CA: Sage, 2009.

Denton-Borhaug, Kelly. "'Like Acid Seeping into Your Soul:' Religio-Cultural Violence in Moral Injury." In *Exploring Moral Injury in Sacred Texts*, edited by Joseph McDonald, 111–33. London: Jessica Kingsley, 2017.

———. "Moral Injury, the Bible and US War-Culture." In *Moral Injury: A Guidebook for Understanding and Engagement*, edited by Brad E. Kelle, 173–88. Lanham, MD: Lexington, 2020.

———. *And Then Your Soul Is Gone: Moral Injury and U.S. War-Culture*. Sheffield, UK: Equinox, 2021.

Doehring, Carrie. "The Challenges of Being Bilingual: Methods of Integrating Psychological and Religious Studies." In *Understanding Pastoral Counseling*, edited by Elizabeth A. Maynard and Jill L. Snodgrass, 87–99. New York: Springer, 2015.

———. "Military Moral Injury: An Evidence-Based and Intercultural Approach to Spiritual Care." In *Military Moral Injury and Spiritual Care*, edited by Nancy J. Ramsay and Carrie Doehring, 20–41. St. Louis: Chalice, 2019.

———. *The Practice of Pastoral Care: A Postmodern Approach*. Revised and expanded ed. Louisville, KY: Westminster John Knox, 2015.

BIBLIOGRAPHY

Driedger, Patricia Morrison. "Different Lyrics but the Same Tune: Multifaith Spiritual Care in a Canadian Context." In *Interfaith Spiritual Care: Understandings and Practices,* edited by Daniel S. Schipani and Leah Dawn Bueckert, 129–42. Kitchener, ON: Pandora, 2009.

Dunn, James D. G. *The Theology of Paul the Apostle.* Grand Rapids: Eerdmans, 1998.

Engelmann, Kim V. *Running in Circles: How False Spirituality Traps Us in Unhealthy Relationships.* Downers Grove, IL: Intervarsity, 2007.

Entwistle, David N. *Integrative Approaches to Psychology and Christianity: An Introduction to Worldview Issues, Philosophical Foundations, and Models of Integration.* 4th ed. Eugene: Cascade, 2021.

Erikson, Erik H. *The Life Cycle Completed: A Review.* New York: W.W. Norton, 1982.

Federschmidt, Karl, Eberhard Hauschildt, Christoph Schneider-Harpprecht, Klaus Temme, and Helmut Weiß, eds. *Handbuch Interkulturelle Seelsorge.* Neukirchen-Vluyn, Germany: Neukirchener Verlag, 2002.

Federschmidt, Karl, and Daniel Louw, eds. *Intercultural and Interreligious Pastoral Caregiving: The SIPCC 1995-2015: 20 Years of International Practice and Reflection.* Norderstedt, Germany: Gesellschaft für Interkulturelle Seelsorge und Beratung/Society for Intercultural Pastoral Care and Counseling, 2015.

Feldman, Deborah. *Unorthodox: The Scandalous Rejection of My Hasidic Roots.* New York: Simon & Schuster, 2012.

Fernandez, Eleazar S., ed. *Threshold Dwellers in the Age of Global Pandemic.* Eugene: Pickwick, 2022.

Fiddes, Paul S. *Seeing the World and Knowing God: Hebrew Wisdom and Christian Doctrine in a Late-Modern Context.* Oxford: Oxford University Press, 2013.

Fitchett, George, and Steve Nolan, eds. *Case Studies in Spiritual Care: Healthcare Chaplaincy Assessments, Interventions, and Outcomes.* London: Jessica Kingsley, 2018.

———, eds. *Spiritual Care in Practice: Case Studies in Healthcare Chaplaincy.* London: Jessica Kingsley, 2015.

Fitchett, George, Kelsey B. White, and Kathryn Lyndes. *Evidenced-Based Healthcare Chaplaincy: A Research Reader.* London: Jessica Kingsley, 2018.

Foster, Charles R., et al. *Educating Clergy: Teaching Practices and Pastoral Imagination.* San Francisco: Jossey-Bass, 2006.

Foster, Richard J. *Streams of Living Water: Essential Practices from the Six Great Traditions of Christian Faith.* San Francisco: Harper and Row, 1998.

Fowler, James W. *Faith Development and Pastoral Care.* Philadelphia: Fortress, 1987.

———. *Stages of Faith: The Psychology of Human Development and the Quest for Meaning.* San Francisco: Harper, 1981.

Friedman, Dayle A., ed. *Jewish Pastoral Care: A Practical Handbook from Traditional and Contemporary Sources.* 2nd ed. Woodstock: Jewish Lights, 2005.

Friedman, Michelle, and Rachel Yehuda. *The Art of Jewish Pastoral Counseling: A Guide for All Faiths.* London and New York: Routledge, 2017.

Fritsche, Sally. "An Atheist's Prayer." July 9, 2017, Follen Community Church, Lexington, MA. https://news-archive.hds.harvard.edu/news/2017/07/17/sally-fritche-atheists-prayer.

Gabriel, Victor, and Duane R. Bidwell. "Leading and Facilitating Spiritual Reflection." In *Chaplaincy and Spiritual Care in the Twenty-First Century,* edited by Wendy Cadge and Shelly Rambo, 90–109. Chapel Hill: University of North Carolina Press, 2022.

BIBLIOGRAPHY

Giles, Cheryl A., & Willa B. Miller, eds. *The Arts of Contemplative Care: Pioneering Voices in Buddhist Chaplaincy and Pastoral Work.* Somerville, MA: Wisdom, 2012.

Gorski, Philip S., and Samuel L. Perry. *The Flag and the Cross: White Christian Nationalism and the Threat to American Democracy.* Oxford: Oxford University Press, 2022.

Graham, Elaine, et al. *Theological Reflection: Methods.* 2nd ed. London: SCM, 2019.

Graham, Larry K. *Moral Injury: Restoring Wounded Souls.* Nashville: Abingdon, 2017.

Grefe, Dagmar. *Encounters for Change: Interreligious Cooperation in the Care of Individuals and Communities.* Eugene, OR: Wipf & Stock, 2011.

Greider, Kathleen. "Religious Location and Counseling: Engaging Diversity and Difference in Views of Religion." In *The Art of Spiritual Care Across Religious Difference*, edited by Jill L. Snodgrass, 17–53. Minneapolis: Fortress, 2024.

Griffith, James L. *Religion That Heals, Religion That Harms: A Guide for Clinical Practice.* New York: Guilford, 2010.

Gritsch, Eric W. *Toxic Spirituality: Four Enduring Temptations of Christian Faith.* 2nd ed. Minneapolis: Fortress, 2009.

Guinn, Jeff. *The Road to Jonestown: Jim Jones and Peoples Temple.* New York: Simon & Schuster, 2017.

Gülen, Fethullah. *Emerald Hills of the Heart: Key Concepts in the Practice of Sufism.* Istanbul: Tughra, 2004.

Hall, Stephen S. *Wisdom: From Philosophy to Neuroscience.* New York: Knopf, 2010.

Handzo, George F., et al. "Outcomes for Professional Health Care Chaplaincy: An International Call to Action." *Journal of Health Care Chaplaincy* 20 (2014), 43–53.

Harper, Douglas. "Pandemic (adj.)." *Online Etymology Dictionary.* https://www.etymonline.com/word/pandemic#etymonline_v_3061

Harris, Maria. *Teaching and Religious Imagination: An Essay in the Theology of Teaching.* San Francisco: Harper & Row, 1987.

Heller Levitt, Dana, and Holly J. Hartwig Moorhead, eds. *Values and Ethics in Counseling: Real-Life Ethical Decision Making.* New York: Routledge, 2013.

Hendricks, Obery M., Jr. *Christians Against Christianity: How Right-Wing Evangelicals Are Destroying Our Nation and Our Faith.* Boston: Beacon, 2021.

Hodge, David R. *Spiritual Assessment in Social Work and Mental Health Practice.* New York: Columbia University Press, 2015.

Hodgson, Peter C. *God's Wisdom: Toward a Theology of Education.* Louisville, KY: Westminster John Knox, 1999.

Holeman, Virginia Todd. *Theology for Better Counseling: Trinitarian Foundations for Healing and Formation.* Downers Grove, IL: InterVarsity, 2012.

Hood, Ralph W., Jr., et al. *The Psychology of Religious Fundamentalism.* New York: Guilford, 2005.

Hunsinger, Deborah van Deusen. "An Interdisciplinary Map for Christian Counselors: Theology and Psychology in Pastoral Counseling." In *Care for the Soul: Exploring the Intersection of Psychology and Theology*, edited by Mark R. McMinn and Timothy R. Phillips, 218–40. Downers Grove, IL: InterVarsity, 2001.

———. *Theology and Pastoral Counseling: A New Interdisciplinary Approach.* Grand Rapids: Eerdmans, 1995.

Hutt, Karen L., ed. *The Call to Care: Essays by Unitarian Universalist Chaplains.* Boston: Skinner, 2016.

Intercultural Development Inventory. "About Us." https://www.idiinventory.com/about-us

BIBLIOGRAPHY

International Association for Spiritual Care. "Mission Statement." https://ia-sc.org/mission-statement/

Isgandarova, Nazila. "The Correlational Approach to Islamic Spiritual Care." *Tidsskrift om Islam & Christendom* 1 (2019), 15–28.

———. *Islamic Spiritual and Religious Care: Theory and Practices*. Kitchener, ON: Pandora, 2018.

———. *Muslim Women, Domestic Violence, and Psychotherapy: Theological and Clinical Issues*. New York: Routledge, 2019.

Jones, Russell Siler. *Spirit in Session: Working with Your Client's Spirituality (and Your Own) in Psychotherapy*. West Conshohocken, PA: Templeton, 2019.

Keddie, Tony. *Republican Jesus: How the Right Has Rewritten the Gospels*. Oakland: University of California Press, 2020.

Kelle, Brad E. *The Bible and Moral Injury: Reading Scripture Alongside War's Unseen Wounds*. Nashville: Abingdon, 2020.

———, ed. *Moral Injury: A Guidebook for Understanding and Engagement*. Lanham, MD: Lexington, 2020.

Keyes, Corey L. M., and Jonathan Haidt, eds. *Flourishing: Positive Psychology and the Life Well-Lived*. Washington, DC: American Psychological Association, 2002.

Khatab, Sayed. *Understanding Islamic Fundamentalism: The Theological and Ideological Basis of al-Qa'ida's Political Tactics*. Cairo: American University in Cairo Press, 2011.

Kobes Du Mez, Kristin. *Jesus and John Wayne: How White Evangelicals Corrupted a Faith and Fractured a Nation*. New York: Liveright, 2020.

Koenig, Harold G., et al. *Handbook of Religion and Health*. 2nd ed. Oxford: Oxford University Press, 2012.

Koestler, Arthur. *The Act of Creation*. London: Hutchinson, 1964.

Kornfield, Jack. *The Wise Heart: A Guide to the Universal Teachings of Buddhist Psychology*. New York: Bantam, 2008.

Kraybill, Donald B., et al. *Amish Grace: How Forgiveness Transcended Tragedy*. San Francisco: Jossey-Bass, 2007.

———. *The Amish Way: Patient Faith in a Perilous World*. San Francisco: Jossey-Bass, 2010.

Kruizinga, Renske, et al. *Learning from Case Studies in Chaplaincy: Towards Practice Based Evidence and Professionalism*. Utrecht, The Netherlands: Eburon, 2020.

Kruse, Kevin M. *One Nation Under God: How Corporate America Invented Christian America*. New York: Basic, 2015.

Kruse, Kevin M., and Julian E. Zelizer, eds. *Myth America: Historians Take on the Biggest Legends and Lies About Our Past*. New York: Basic, 2023.

LaCugna, Catherine Mowry. *God for Us: The Trinity and Christian Life*. San Francisco: Harper, 1991.

LaMothe, Ryan. *Care of Soul, Care of Polis: Toward a Political Pastoral Theology*. Eugene, OR: Cascade, 2018.

———. *A Radical Political Theology for the Anthropocene Era: Thinking and Being Otherwise*. Eugene, OR: Cascade, 2021.

Lartey, Emmanuel Y. *In Living Color: An Intercultural Approach to Pastoral Care and Counseling*, 2nd ed. London: Jessica Kingsley, 2003.

Lechner, Frank J. "Fundamentalism." In *Encyclopedia of Religion and Society*, edited by William H. Swatos, Jr., 197–200. Walnut Creek, CA: AltaMira, 1998.

Bibliography

Lee, Bandy. *The Dangerous Case of Donald Trump: 37 Psychiatrists and Mental Health Experts Assess a President*. New York: Thomas Dunne, 2019.

Levine, Amy-Jill. *The Difficult Words of Jesus: A Beginner's Guide to His Most Perplexing Teachings*. Nashville: Abingdon, 2021.

———. *Sermon on the Mount: A Beginner's Guide to the Kingdom of Heaven*. Nashville: Abingdon, 2020.

———. *Short Stories by Jesus: The Enigmatic Parables of a Controversial Rabbi*. New York: HarperCollins, 2014.

Levine, Martin. *The Positive Psychology of Buddhism and Yoga: Paths to A Mature Happiness*. New York: Psychology, 2000.

Levitz, Yisrael N., and Abraham J. Twerski, eds. *A Practical Guide to Rabbinic Counseling*. Woodstock, VT: Jewish Lights, 2012.

Liefbroer, Anke I. *Interfaith Spiritual Care*. PhD thesis, VU University Amsterdam, 2020.

Loder, James E. *The Transforming Moment*. 2nd ed. Colorado Springs: Helmers and Howard, 1989.

Lopez, Shane J., and C.R. Snyder, eds. *The Oxford Handbook of Positive Psychology*. 2nd ed. Oxford: Oxford University Press, 2011.

Mabry, John R., ed. *Spiritual Guidance Across Religions: A Sourcebook for Spiritual Directors and Other Professionals Providing Counsel to People of Differing Faith Traditions*. Woodstock, VT: SkyLight Paths, 2014.

Malony, H. Newton, and David W. Augsburger. *Christian Counseling: An Introduction*. Nashville: Abingdon, 2007.

Mauldin, Jane Ellen. "Inherent Worth and Dignity." In *The Call to Care: Essays by Unitarian Universalist Chaplains*, edited by Karen L. Hutt, 1–15. Boston: Skinner, 2016.

May, Rollo. *The Courage to Create*. New York: Norton, 1975.

Maynard, Elizabeth A., and Jill L. Snodgrass, eds. *Understanding Pastoral Counseling*. New York: Springer, 2015.

McDonald, Joseph, ed. *Exploring Moral Injury in Sacred Texts*. London: Jessica Kingsley, 2017.

McKellar, Melody A., and Roger Armitte. "Journey toward Creator and the Realm of Peace." In *Multifaith Views in Spiritual Care*, edited by Daniel Schipani, 15–30. Kitchener, ON: Pandora, 2013.

McMinn, Mark R. *Psychology, Theology, and Spirituality in Christian Counseling*. Wheaton: Tyndale, 1996.

McMinn, Mark R., and Timothy R. Phillips, eds. *Care for the Soul: Exploring the Intersection of Psychology and Theology*. Downers Grove, IL: InterVarsity, 2001.

Meagher, Robert Emmet. *Killing from the Inside Out: Moral Injury and Just War*. Eugene, OR: Wipf & Stock, 2014.

Meagher, Robert Emmet, and Douglas A. Pryer, eds. *War and Moral Injury: A Reader*. Eugene, OR: Wipf & Stock, 2018.

Mercadante, Linda A. *Belief without Borders: Inside the Minds of the Spiritual but not Religious*. New York: Oxford University Press, 2014.

Michon, Nathan Jishin, and Daniel Clarkson Fisher, eds. *A Thousand Hands: A Guidebook to Caring for Your Buddhist Community*. Manotick, ON: Sumeru, 2014.

Mikva, Rachel S. *Dangerous Religious Ideas: The Deep Roots of Self-Critical Faith in Judaism, Christianity, and Islam*. Boston: Beacon, 2020.

Miller, William R., ed. *Integrating Spirituality into Treatment: Resources for Practitioners*. Washington, DC: American Psychological Association, 1999.

Bibliography

Miller-McLemore, Bonnie J. *Christian Theology in Practice: Discovering a Discipline.* Grand Rapids: Eerdmans, 2012.

Moon, Hellena, and Emmanuel Y. Lartey, eds. *Postcolonial Practices of Care: A Project of Togetherness during COVID-19 and Racial Violence.* Eugene, OR: Pickwick, 2022.

Moon, Zachary. *Coming Home: Ministry That Matters with Veterans and Military Families.* St. Louis: Chalice, 2015.

———. *Warriors Between Worlds: Moral Injury and Identities in Crisis.* Lanham, MD: Lexington, 2019.

Moore, S. K. *Military Chaplains as Agents of Peace: Religious Leader Engagement in Conflict and Post-Conflict Environments.* Toronto: Lexington, 2012.

Morgan, Jonathan, and Steven J. Sandage. "A Developmental Model for Interreligious Competence." *Archive for the Psychology of Religion* 38 (2016), 129–58.

Moriarti, Glendon L., ed. *Integrating Faith and Psychology: Twelve Psychologists Tell Their Stories.* Downers Grove, IL: InterVarsity, 2010.

Murphy, Roland E. *The Tree of Life: An Exploration of Biblical Wisdom Literature.* New York: Doubleday, 1990.

Nawaz, Maajid. *Radical: My Journey Out of Islamist Extremism.* Lanham, MD: Lyons, 2013.

Nelson, Anne. *Shadow Network: Media, Money, and the Secret Hub of the Radical Right.* New York: Bloomsbury, 2019.

Nolan, Steve, and Annelieke Damen, eds. *Transforming Chaplaincy: The George Fitchett Reader.* Eugene, OR: Pickwick, 2021.

Norberg, Tilda. *Consenting to Grace: An Introduction to Gestalt Pastoral Care.* Staten Island, NY: Penn House, 2005.

Noth, Isabelle, and Claudia Kohli Reichenbach, eds. *Pastoral and Spiritual Care Across Religions and Cultures II: Spiritual Care and Migration.* Götingen, Germany: Vandenhoeck & Ruprecht, 2019.

Ochs, Peter. *Religion without Violence: The Practice and Philosophy of Scriptural Reasoning.* Eugene, OR: Cascade, 2019.

O'Connor, Kathleen M. *The Wisdom Literature.* Wilmington: Michael Glazier, 1988.

Olson, R. Paul. *Religious Theories of Personality and Psychotherapy: East Meets West.* New York: Haworth, 2002.

Onishi, Bradley. *Preparing for War: The Extremist History of White Christian Nationalism—And What Comes Next.* Minneapolis: Broadleaf, 2023.

Osmer, Richard R. *Practical Theology: An Introduction.* Grand Rapids: Eerdmans, 2008.

Pargament, Kenneth I, ed. *APA Handbook of Psychology, Religion, and Spirituality.* Washington, DC: American Psychological Association, 2013.

———. *The Psychology of Religion and Coping: Theory, Research, Practice.* New York: Guilford, 1997.

———. *Spiritually Integrated Psychology: Understanding and Addressing the Sacred.* New York: Guilford, 2007.

Pargament, Kenneth I., and Julie J. Exline. "Shaken to the Core: Understanding and Addressing Spiritual Struggles in Psychotherapy." In *Handbook of Spiritually Integrated Psychotherapies*, edited by P. Scott Richards, G. E. Kawika Allen, and Daniel K. Judd, 119–34. Washington, DC: American Psychological Association, 2023.

———. *Working with Spiritual Struggles in Psychotherapy: From Research to Practice.* New York: Guilford, 2022.

BIBLIOGRAPHY

Parker, Alan, dir. *Evita*. 1996; Burbank, CA: Hollywood Pictures. DVD.
Partridge, Christopher H., ed. *Fundamentalisms*. Carlisle, UK: Paternoster, 2001.
Pasquale, Teresa B. *Sacred Wounds: A Path to Healing from Spiritual Trauma*. St. Louis: Chalice, 2015.
Pearce, M. J., et al. "A Novel Training Program for Mental Health Providers in Religious and Spiritual Competencies." *Spirituality in Clinical Practice* 6, no. 2 (2019), 73–82.
Peck, M. Scott. *People of the Lie: The Hope for Healing Human Evil*. New York: Simon & Schuster, 1998.
Pedersen, Paul B., Walter J. Lonner, Juris G. Draguns, Joseph E. Trimble, and Maria R. Scharrón-del Río, eds. *Counseling Across Cultures*. 7th ed. Los Angeles: SAGE, 2016.
Penchansky, David. *Understanding Wisdom Literature: Conflict and Dissonance in the Hebrew Text*. Grand Rapids: Eerdmans, 2012.
Perdue, Leo G. *Wisdom and Creation: The Theology of Wisdom Literature*. Nashville: Abingdon, 1994.
Peterson, Christopher, and Martin E. P. Seligman. *Character Strengths and Virtues*. Washington, DC: American Psychological Association, 2004.
Phelps-Roper, Megan. *Unfollow: A Memoir of Loving and Leaving the Westboro Baptist Church*. New York: Farrar, Straus and Giroux, 2019.
Plante, Thomas G. *Spiritual Practices in Psychotherapy: Thirteen Tools for Enhancing Psychological Health*. Washington, DC: American Psychological Association, 2009.
Poling, James Newton. *Deliver Us from Evil: Resisting Racial and Gender Oppression*. Minneapolis: Fortress, 1996.
Quack, Johannes, Cora Schuh, and Susanne Kind. *The Diversity of Nonreligion: Normativities and Contested Relations*. New York: Routledge, 2020.
Ramsay, Nancy J., and Carrie Doehring, eds. *Military Moral Injury and Spiritual Care: A Resource for Religious Leaders and Professional Caregivers*. St. Louis: Chalice, 2019.
Rassool, G. Husein. *Islamic Counselling: An Introduction to Theory and Practice*. London: Routledge, 2016.
Richards, P. Scott, G.E. Kawika Allen, and Daniel K. Judd, eds. *Handbook of Spiritually Integrated Psychotherapies*. Washington, DC: American Psychological Association, 2023.
Richards, P. Scott, and Allen E. Bergin, eds. *Handbook of Psychotherapy and Religious Diversity*. 2nd ed. Washington, DC: American Psychological Association, 2014.
———. *A Spiritual Strategy for Counseling and Psychotherapy*. 2nd ed. Washington, DC: American Psychological Association, 2005.
Roberts, Robert C., and Mark R. Talbot, eds. *Limning the Psyche: Explorations in Christian Psychology*. Grand Rapids: Eerdmans, 1997.
Rogers-Vaughn, Bruce. "Best Practices in Pastoral Counseling: Is Theology Necessary?" *Journal of Pastoral Theology* 23, no. 1 (2013), 2–24.
———. *Caring for Souls in a Neoliberal Age*. New York: Palgrave Macmillan, 2016.
Rothman, Abdallah. *Developing a Model of Islamic Psychology and Psychotherapy*. New York: Routledge, 2022.
Sandage, Steven J., and Jeannine K. Brown. *Relational Integration of Psychology and Christian Theology: Theory, Research, and Practice*. New York: Routledge, 2018.
Sandage, Steven J., and Brad D. Strawn, eds. *Spiritual Diversity in Psychotherapy: Engaging the Sacred in Clinical Practice*. Washington D.C.: American Psychological Association, 2022.

BIBLIOGRAPHY

Sanford, Monica. "Buddhist Practical Theology: Methods for Putting Wisdom into Practice." In *A Thousand Hands: A Guidebook to Caring for Your Buddhist Community*, edited by Nathan Jishin Michon and Daniel Clarkson Fisher, 55–63. Manotick, ON: Sumeru, 2014.

———. *Kalyanamitra: A Model for Buddhist Spiritual Care, Volume 1*. Manotick, ON: Sumeru, 2021.

———. "Secret Atheist: Internal and External Tensions Affecting Buddhists as Interreligious Caregiving Professionals." In *Navigating Religious Difference in Spiritual Care and* Counseling, edited by Jill L. Snodgrass, 213–41. Minneapolis: Fortress, 2024.

Scazzero, Peter. *Emotionally Healthy Spirituality*. Grand Rapids: Zondervan, 2017.

Schipani, Daniel S. "Biblical Foundations: Challenges and Possibilities of Interfaith Caregiving." In *Interfaith Spiritual Care: Understandings and Practices*, edited by Daniel S. Schipani and Leah D. Bueckert, 51–77. Kitchener, ON: Pandora, 2009.

———. "Case Study Method." In *The Wiley-Blackwell Companion to Practical Theology*, edited by Bonnie J. Miller-McLemore, 91–101. Malden: Blackwell, 2013.

———. "Fundamentalism as Toxic Spirituality: Exploring the Psycho-Spiritual Structure and Dynamics of Violent Extremism." In *Teaching in a World of Violent Extremism*, edited by Eleazar S. Fernandez, 178–207. Eugene, OR: Wipf & Stock, 2021.

———. "The Heart of the Matter: Engaging the Spirit in Spiritual Care." In *Multifaith Views in Spiritual Care*, edited by Daniel S. Schipani, 149–66. Kitchener, ON: Pandora, 2013.

———, ed. *Multifaith Views in Spiritual Care*. Kitchener, ON: Pandora, 2013.

———. "Pastoral and Spiritual Care in Multifaith Contexts." In *Teaching for a Multifaith World*, edited by Eleazar S. Fernandez, 124–46. Eugene, OR: Wipf & Stock, 2017.

———. "Transformation in Intercultural Bible Reading: A View from Practical Theology." In *Bible and Transformation: The Promise of Intercultural Bible Reading*, edited by Hans de Wit and Janet Dyk, 99–116. Atlanta: SBL, 2015.

———. *The Way of Wisdom in Pastoral Counseling*. Elkhart, IN: Institute of Mennonite Studies, 2003.

Schipani, Daniel S., and Leah D. Bueckert, eds. *Interfaith Spiritual Care: Understandings and Practices*. Kitchener, ON: Pandora, 2009.

Schipani, Daniel S., Martin Walton, and Dominiek Lootens, eds. *Where Are We?: Pastoral Environments and Care for Migrants—Intercultural and Interreligious Perspectives*. Mishawaka, IN: Duley, 2018.

Schneider, Kirk J., J. Fraser Pierson, and James F. T. Bugental, eds. *The Handbook of Humanist Psychology: Theory, Research, and Practice*. 2nd ed. Thousand Oakes, CA: Sage, 2015.

Schrock, Dan. *A Spiritual Health Inventory*. http://www.danschrock.org/inventory.aspx.

Seidel, Andrew L. *The Founding Myth: Why Christian Nationalism Is Un-American*. New York: Union Square & Co., 2019.

Sider, Ronald J., ed. *The Spiritual Danger of Donald Trump: 30 Evangelical Christians on Justice, Truth, and Moral Integrity*. Eugene, OR: Cascade, 2020.

Snodgrass, Jill, ed. *The Art of Spiritual Care Across Religious Difference*. Minneapolis: Fortress Press, 2024.

Society for Intercultural Pastoral Care and Counselling. "Mission Statement and Self-Understanding." https://sipcc.org/mission-statement/mission-statement/mission-statement

BIBLIOGRAPHY

Sternberg, Robert J., and Judith Glück, eds. *The Cambridge Handbook on Wisdom*. Cambridge: Cambridge University Press, 2019.

———, eds. *The Psychology of Wisdom*. Cambridge: Cambridge University Press, 2022.

Stewart, Katherine. *The Power Worshippers: Inside the Dangerous Rise of Religious Nationalism*. New York: Bloomsbury, 2020.

Stone, Howard W., and James O. Duke. *How to Think Theologically*. 3rd ed. Minneapolis: Fortress, 2013.

Sue, Derald Wing, et al. *Counseling the Culturally Diverse*. 9th ed. Hoboken, NJ: Wiley, 2022.

Sutton, Nicholas, et al. *Hindu Chaplaincy*. Oxford: Oxford Centre for Hindu Studies, 2017.

Swinton, John, and Harriet Mowat. *Practical Theology and Qualitative Research*. 2nd ed. London: SCM, 2016.

Thatamanil, John J. *Circling the Elephant: A Comparative Theology of Religious Diversity*. New York: Fordham University Press, 2020.

Tillich, Paul. *The Courage to Be*. New Haven: Yale University Press, 1953.

———. *The Meaning of Health: The Relation of Religion and Health*. Richmond, VA: North Atlantic, 1981.

Tracy, David. *Blessed Rage for Order: The New Pluralism in Theology*. New York: Seabury, 1975.

Unitarian Universalist Association. *Bylaws and Rules as Amended Through May 22, 2023*. https://www.uua.org/uuagovernance/bylaws

Vieten, Cassandra, and Shelley Scammell. *Spiritual and Religious Competencies in Clinical Practice: Guidelines for Psychotherapists and Mental Health Professionals*. Oakland: New Harbinger, 2015.

von Rad, Gerhard. *Wisdom in Israel*. Nashville: Abingdon, 1972.

Walton, Martin. "Encountering Difference: Repertoire of Intercultural and Interreligious Chaplaincy." In *Care, Healing, and Human Well-Being within Interreligious Discourses*, edited by Helmut Weiss, Karl H. Federschmidt, Daniel Louw, and Linda Sauer Bredvik, 51–65. Stellenbosch, South Africa: African Sun Media, 2021.

Weiss, Helmut, Karl H. Federschmidt, Daniel Louw, and Linda Sauer Bredvik, eds. *Care, Healing, and Human Well-Being within Interreligious Discourses*. Stellenbosch, South Africa: African Sun Media, 2021.

Weiß, Helmut, Karl H. Federschmidt, and Klaus Temme, eds. *Handbuch Interreligiöse Seelsorge*. Neukirchen-Vluyn, Germany: Neukirchener Verlag, 2010.

Whitehead, Andrew L. *American Idolatry: How Christian Nationalism Betrays the Gospel and Threatens the Church*. Grand Rapids: Brazos, 2023.

Whitehead, Andrew L., and Samuel L. Perry. *Taking America Back for God: Christian Nationalism in the United States*. Oxford: Oxford University Press, 2020.

Winell, Marlene. *Leaving the Fold: A Guide for Former Fundamentalists and Others Leaving Their Religion*. Oakland: New Harbinger, 1993.

Wintz, Susan K., and George Handzo. *Handbook: Patients' Spiritual and Cultural Values for Health Care Professionals*. New York: HealthCare Chaplaincy Network, 2014. https://dspd.utah.gov/wp-content/uploads/2020/11/cultural_sensitivity_handbook_from_healthcare_chaplaincy_network.pdf

Witherington, Ben, III. *Jesus the Sage: The Pilgrimage of Wisdom*. Minneapolis: Fortress, 1993.

World Health Organization. "WHO COVID-19 Dashboard." https://data.who.int/dashboards/covid19/cases?n=c.

www.ingramcontent.com/pod-product-compliance
Lightning Source LLC
Chambersburg PA
CBHW072146160426
43197CB00012B/2274